THE LUMP

 A Gynecologist's Journey *with* Male Breast Cancer

ALAN JOHNS, MD

LIVE OAK
BOOK COMPANY

www.liveoakbookcompany.com

Published by Live Oak Book Company
Austin, TX
www.liveoakbookcompany.com

Distributed by Live Oak Book Company

For ordering information or special discounts for bulk purchases, please contact Live Oak Book Company at PO Box 91869, Austin, TX 78709, 512.891.6100.

Design and composition by Greenleaf Book Group LLC
Cover design by Greenleaf Book Group LLC

Publisher's Cataloging-In-Publication Data
(Prepared by The Donohue Group, Inc.)
Johns, Alan, MD
    The lump : a gynecologist's journey with male breast cancer / Alan Johns.— 1st ed.
        p. ; cm.
    Available also as an ebook.
    ISBN: 978-1-936909-00-1
    1. Johns, Alan, MD—Health. 2. Breast—Cancer—Patients—Biography. 3. Cancer in men—United States—Biography. 4. Gynecologists—United States—Biography. 5. Breast cancer patients' writings, American. I. Title.
RC279.6.J65 J65 2011
616.994/49/0092   2011927178

Print ISBN: 978-1-936909-00-1
eBook ISBN: 978-1-936909-01-8

First Edition

CONTENTS

CHAPTER ONE

June 9, 1998

It seemed to happen so quickly.

The day was clear and crisp—a spring day—and normally I'd have felt happy to be alive. But the tiny kernel of worry that had been plaguing me since I'd gone for the biopsy rubbed against my usual optimistic attitude, and I couldn't think about anything but the phone call I was expecting. What would the doctor say when he gave me the results? I shook the question away, told myself for the hundredth time that everything was going to be all right. I had a perfect life: a challenging profession that I loved, a busy medical practice, a teaching appointment at a major medical school, an international reputation. I had opportunities at every turn.

Plus, my personal life was in good order. My two daughters were successful and healthy, I loved my wife, and we had a great home in Fort Worth, Texas. For a guy from Graham, Texas, life had been much better than I'd expected.

So on that day, whenever the worry sneaked into my thoughts, I brushed it away by telling myself that I'd ignored "it" (I could never think of the mass I'd found as "the lump") for such a long time, another day would be easy. Besides, I was a doctor. Bad things happened to patients, not doctors. OK, maybe bad things happened to doctors sometimes, but to *other* doctors, not to me.

About 11 a.m. I was talking with a patient in examining room number one. Actually, "Mrs. Smith" (as I'll call her), who was fifty-three years old at the time, was doing the talking, and I was trying to concentrate on her complaints. I'd been her gynecologist for years, delivered her two children, performed her hysterectomy, and had supported her as she traversed a messy divorce. She needed support again on this visit. She was an emotional wreck as she complained that she was gaining weight, her hair was falling out, she had no energy, she was fighting hot flashes, and she couldn't sleep. Through my years of treating Mrs. Smith, I knew she just needed to talk to someone who was nonjudgmental.

I nodded with true sympathy, listening carefully, yet I desperately wanted to move on to my next patient, who would distract me from thinking about the phone call I was expecting any minute. This next patient had a very interesting ovarian mass. For a surgeon, nothing is quite as fascinating as a mass in a body cavity. Maybe it's because a tumor can be cut out—something can be done. Other than listen, there wasn't much I could do for Mrs. Smith's broken family life.

I concentrated on what she was saying, even though my mind kept wandering back to *my* doctor and what he was going to tell me. I was anxious to get the good news I fully expected would come, forget about my imagined medical problem, and move on with my life.

Right between Mrs. Smith's words "I can't" and "sleep," it happened. My receptionist's voice sounded louder and more shrill than usual, as if she were screaming over the office intercom: "Dr. Johns, a doctor for you on line one."

Damn. Immediately I began to sweat. I babbled some excuse to Mrs. Smith and quickly left the examining room. Nervously I ducked into my office, shut the door, took a deep breath, and picked up the phone, hoping it was a friend calling about a golf game.

But Fred's distinctive "hello" told me this phone call wouldn't be about tee times. My heart began to beat faster, and I felt dizzy, deathly cold, and panicked. I fought the urge to hang up and go back to my day, and instead sat at my desk.

"I'm sorry, Alan. It's an invasive ductal cell carcinoma." Fred sounded as if he were talking in slow motion, the syllables elongated, his voice dull and scary—like a death knell.

Ductal cell carcinoma—breast cancer, damn, breast cancer. My mind went blank as terror washed over me and overwhelmed my thoughts.

Without saying a word, I slammed down the phone as if that blend of plastic, vinyl, and wire were personally responsible for what I had just heard. My diagnosis wouldn't exist if I didn't hear any more about it. I stared at the phone and told myself I had to get control—I was a doctor and should be able to handle this. I'd taken a lot of these calls from my pathologist colleagues, but they were about breast cancer in someone else, usually someone female—not me. These calls were never about benign results; doctors don't call about normal stuff because they don't have time. If I got a call, the news was never good.

I always prided myself on keeping a somewhat detached, professional attitude with the bad-news calls. I'd listen carefully to the diagnosis and ask detailed questions, making absolutely certain I understood what I was being told. When necessary, I did research on the diagnosis and alternatives for treatment. Next, my nurses and I would spend time deciding how to break the news to our patients in the least alarming, most hopeful ways possible. We considered a lot of things before making these calls: age, personality, family and job situation, medical problems, and a host of other variables.

We never phoned the patient late in the day or on a Friday. I knew there was nothing quite as unnerving as having an entire weekend to worry and imagine the worst. I always wanted my patients to have the option of coming directly to the office to talk as soon as they wanted or needed to. I took pride in being there to care for and comfort my patients.

I took a deep breath. Now I was the patient and I'd just slammed down the phone. I, the one who was always prepared for bad news and always reacted professionally.

In those brief seconds my life had turned upside down.

I broke into another cold sweat. What had happened to the confident, even cocky, surgeon I thought I knew? In his place sat a terrified patient, his worst fears realized.

I leaned forward, placed my elbows on the desk, and rested my head in my hands as more cold chills attacked me. As if in a dream, I thought I could feel the cancer spreading into my lungs and liver. The absurd thought made me dizzier, more lightheaded, so I didn't dare stand. Suddenly, for the first time in my life, I wondered what in the hell had gone wrong. What was it going to feel like to die?

CHAPTER TWO

Graham

Graham, Texas, was an improbable starting point for my career in surgery, but that's where it began. In 1948, the year I was born, Graham, in north-central Texas, was a small, sleepy community boasting a population of about nine thousand. Most of the townspeople were typical southerners: friendly, churchgoing residents with conservative views.

I spent quite a few of my Sunday afternoons dove hunting with my father, my grandfather, and their friends. When I was five, my dad and grandfather taught me to shoot a shotgun and hunt mourning dove. Dove season began September 1 and ran through the end of November, and bird hunting on Sunday afternoon after church was a small-town ritual back then. My mom and dad were married on September 1 (the opening day of dove season), and Mom claimed that the only September 1 she ever saw my dad was their wedding day.

While dove hunting, I watched my dad's friends drink their Wild Turkey whiskey along with a few beers while telling some of the worst jokes I ever heard, all within a few hours of the last "amen" of Sunday morning services. These same men attended our Baptist church and proclaimed the evils of alcohol every Sunday morning. It was all interesting, but as a child I never saw the hypocrisy in a lot of things that went on in my small hometown.

Our family got its start in Graham in 1933, when my dad, Haskel, dropped out of the eighth grade, left his family in Oklahoma, and moved to Graham so he could work with his uncle, Perry Johns. "Uncle Perry" was building a small grocery store in Graham from the ground up, and dad helped him erect the two-thousand-square-foot, cinder-block building at the corner of Fourth and Virginia streets, directly across from the Sinclair gas station. From the time the store opened, it was known as Johns Grocery. The store was a friendly place where everyone knew everyone, and my dad spent the rest of his life building and maintaining that business.

Shortly after arriving in Graham, Dad met Frieda—my mom— and they were married a couple of years later, in 1941, when she finished high school. Early in their marriage Mom worked in a photography studio, using oil-based paint to hand-color portraits taken with black-and-white film. She loved the work and was quite skilled, but the development of color film in the 1950s ended that job. No one needed photographs painted any longer. In the 1960s she took a job at the local Montgomery Ward catalogue store. She ultimately became the store manager, a position she held until the demise of the parent company forced the store's closure in the 1990s.

When World War II started, Dad enlisted in the Coast Guard. He didn't have many war stories; he and his buddies drank a lot of beer while eagerly awaiting the arrival of the Germans and Japanese in the Florida Keys. They were ready, but the invasion never happened, so he came back to Graham. By this time Dad had quit drinking, but unfortunately he kept smoking cigarettes because he believed they helped his asthma. He went back to work at Johns Grocery and learned the meat-cutting trade.

By the time I was thirteen, he was the local butcher in that corner grocery store. Then, because of declining health, Uncle Perry sold the business (but not the building) to my dad and Jesse Fletcher, a friend of my dad's who had worked at the Safeway grocery on the other side of town. They spent a few weekends painting and cleaning up the interior, renamed it Johns & Fletcher Food Store, and opened for business in 1958.

My father and Jesse were improbable partners: a Southern Baptist deacon and a Church of Christ elder. I don't think they ever talked politics or religion, but they worked six and a half days a week and built the business into a local icon, "Johns & Fletcher, the Dollar Stretcher." For the next nineteen years, the two worked together for twelve hours a day, six days a week. They solved problems and shared everything the store could throw at them—and a small-town grocery business generated a hell of a lot of problems.

Sadly, years later both Jesse and my father succumbed to illnesses that were exacerbated by the hard work the grocery business demanded and the stress it caused: Jesse fought hypertension and ultimately lost his battle, and Dad died from his ever-present smoking habit.

But before life took its toll on Dad and Jesse, I grew up in that store. I worked on weekends, first for Uncle Perry, then for my dad and Jesse. I cleaned, swept, mopped floors, stocked shelves, sacked groceries, and boxed eggs. I quickly learned a lot about people, what I wanted out of life, and what it would take to get there.

When I was eight, Dad showed me how to cut up whole chickens, and soon the meat department became my primary focus. I learned to cut up chickens the old-fashioned way, first cutting the drumsticks, then the thighs, the wings, the breasts, and so on. I practiced a lot, and by high school I was competing with the full-time butcher to see who could cut up a chicken the fastest. I usually won because I could cut up a chicken and place it in a container (ready to wrap) in twenty-eight seconds. I nicked a lot of fingers, but I got better and better with a knife.

The meat department at Johns & Fletcher was an old-style butcher shop where a customer went to the counter and asked for a two-and-a-half-inch-thick T-bone steak. We would pull out a big piece of cow, cut the steak by hand, then wrap it in white butcher paper.

Beef was delivered to the store in quarters. Imagine a headless cow split lengthwise and each half split across. These beef quarters were impaled on wicked-looking metal hooks in a big walk-in meat cooler. The front quarters were known as forequarters and the back as hindquarters. Every day we used knives, handsaws, cleavers, and grinders to convert these quarters into burgers, roasts, ribs, and steaks.

Years later, I found that handling those razor-sharp butcher knives wasn't much different than using a scalpel in the operating room; one has to be careful either way.

I became proficient enough with a meat cleaver that I could cut flies in half when they lit on the butcher block. It's a pretty nauseating mental picture, but it was a real challenge for a fifteen-year-old kid, fly hunting with a meat cleaver. When I ultimately became a surgeon, the hand-eye coordination I developed using twelve-inch butcher knives and that meat cleaver served me well.

My experience with the Johns & Fletcher Food Store also taught me what I *didn't* want in life. Dad was continuously trying to squeeze a little money out of a low-profit-margin business while trying to please everyone. Even in a "friendly" small town, folks were demanding, inconsiderate, and demeaning. He was the local grocer, and everyone expected him and Jesse to jump when they wanted something. They usually complied, even to the point of personally delivering fresh eggnog to a wealthy customer on Christmas morning. I hope they thanked him. Dad never said, I never asked, but I doubt they did.

While watching Dad work and worry six days a week, twelve hours a day, I realized that I wanted no part of the grocery business. I didn't care what I did, as long as it wasn't in a grocery store. Yet even then I realized I owed all my determination and work ethic to my father.

Over the years, especially when my sister and I were little, the business occupied most of my father's time and energy, and my mother ended up carrying more than her fair share of the load at home. Besides having the responsibility of a full-time job, she was also keeping house and feeding us. She cooked breakfast, lunch, and dinner seven days a week for my dad, my sister, and me. The three of us just showed up at the kitchen table and ate, never thinking what it had taken to put that meal in front of us. Our only excuse for not helping her: We really didn't know any better. Fifty years later, I realize how viciously unfair this was, but that was pretty much how things worked back then.

As I grew older, staying in Graham after high school was simply not an alternative I was willing to consider. Although he never came directly out and said it, my dad expected nothing less from me than to get the first college degree in our family. During my last two years of high school, we often talked about college during family meals. My dad didn't say much. He just smiled and said he doubted I was smart enough to go to college. This was his gentle, unassuming way of pissing me off and making me work harder. And it worked. I know he was proud of me for completing my education and becoming a physician, but I've always wondered if he was disappointed I chose not to continue the business he had spent his life developing.

As my high school days neared their end, college sounded more and more exciting and would, after all, be a way to get out of Graham and the grocery business. I had no idea what I wanted to do with my life, and medicine wasn't even a distant consideration. But my best friend, Allen, dreamed of being a doctor, and he had access to his parents' new pink Thunderbird, one of the first produced. I loved that car because it gave us—two shy, reserved kids—a sense of freedom. I was an eyeglasses-wearing nerd, but I felt empowered when I was riding around Graham with Allen in the Thunderbird. During these rides we talked a lot about life, college, girls, and doctors. Allen constantly expressed his dream of becoming a doctor, and for hours I listened to him talk about his future in medicine.

To me, "medicine" conjured up images and smells that had been burned into my brain while I sat in our family doc's office in Graham—a nauseating combination of rubbing alcohol, puke, blood, sick kids, and that distinctive odor that old people always seemed to exude as I sat next to them in the waiting room.

I also wanted nothing to do with medicine because I'd watched my Aunt Cora, Uncle Perry's wife, die an excruciatingly prolonged and miserable death from cancer. She spent months lying in bed, wasting away. The unique smell that surrounded her in the last few weeks of her life attacked me every time I visited her. Many years later, I learned it was a combination of dehydration and urea buildup (waste products) in the blood and skin that caused the distinctive "smell of death." Later I also found out that most every doctor recognizes this smell instantaneously.

So when Allen talked about being a doctor, all I could think about were negatives, and I knew that medicine was not in my future.

Finally high school was almost over. Allen and I applied to the

University of Texas–Austin and were accepted. I'm not sure why we decided on UT, but it was state-supported (translation: cheap) and a long way from Graham, so going there seemed like a great idea. After being accepted, we decided to embark on our great adventure by being roommates in one of the older dorms on the Austin campus. Young and enthusiastic, we truly had the world by the tail and were desperately trying to climb on. Our futures could not have looked better.

CHAPTER THREE

Austin

In 1966 the University of Texas had a student population of 28,000, four times larger than the entire town of Graham. My student orientation session was scheduled for mid-August, a few weeks before the fall semester began. When I stepped on campus for the first time, I was stunned by more than just the sheer size of the place.

My orientation came one week after Charles Whitman had killed fourteen people and wounded many more from atop the famous Tower, the centerpiece of the campus. I'll never forget wandering around the campus and finding bullet holes in the granite benches and concrete walkways. As I stared at one of those bullet holes, I remembered my mom's warning: "That place is just too big and dangerous. You should stay closer to home." I was young and thought I was both invincible and smarter than Mom, so I went anyway. But those bullet holes made me wonder if Momma was right.

Weeks later, Allen and I moved into our dorm room on a clear, crisp, beautiful September day. Once all of our belongings were in the room, we couldn't wait for our parents to get the hell out of town. Finally they said their goodbyes, and Allen and I looked out our window. The University of Texas and Austin lay at our feet. We'd finally made it. Wide-eyed and excited didn't come close to describing how we felt. Yet once the excitement began to abate, that "what the hell are we doing here" feeling enveloped us, and "scared shitless" would be a more accurate description of our emotions.

A few days after our move, I declared myself a math major for no specific reason other than that I had done well in high school algebra, geometry, and trigonometry. Even though I didn't have a clue what a math degree would bring me, that major sounded a lot better than working with Allen's sick people and infinitely better than stocking groceries.

The dorm where Allen and I lived was old. It featured community toilets and showers, squeaky wooden floors, no air conditioning, one tiny closet per room, metal bunk beds, and high ceilings with a single light bulb in the center. But we didn't care; to us the dorm was heaven.

Within a month of our arrival I secured a job in the Athletic Cafeteria, a self-contained café for the male scholarship athletes. It was a great job because I was paid one meal for an hour of waiting tables and washing dishes. The best part of my job was that the meal I earned was the same one the jocks ate, and their food was pretty darn good.

Working in the cafeteria was a defining time for me. I got to know the jocks who were the big men on a very big campus. They were friendly, and, to my astonishment, pretty much like me, only bigger, stronger, better looking, and famous. Being around them gave me a real sense of belonging, and during the next four years, I became friends with quite a few of the football players (who won the national championship in 1970) and developed a life-long love for the University of Texas.

That first year I did have worries. Finances were tight, but my cafeteria job helped. My biggest concern, however, was academic failure. I was from a small-town high school, and at UT I was competing with thousands of kids. I was certain most were smarter than I, but I doubted they could outwork me. Because of what I'd learned from my father and the grocery business, I put my head down and worked hard, and my grades reflected my determination.

By my sophomore year I was settled in and vastly more confident. Unfortunately, however, I developed a love for poker. Since I wasn't fearful of flunking out anymore, my grades began to suffer when I discovered partying, poker playing, and beer drinking.

One cool October day, a few hours before a football game, I looked out my open dorm window at Memorial Stadium. UT was having a great football season, and I was euphoric, like every other self-centered college kid. Life could get no better. But as the last endorphin rush abated, it was replaced by a bit of concern. Just what was I going to do with the rest of my life? I'm not sure why that random thought struck me when it did, but it plowed through me like a UT linebacker. Until then I'd never really thought about what my job opportunities would be after I earned my math degree.

It was my best friend Allen's situation that aroused my concern. Around this same time, the Vietnam War was in full swing. Allen couldn't handle the combination of classes, fraternity parties, and old Graham girlfriends, so he dropped out of school, joined the Navy, and became a medic. I missed his friendship, but his actions forced me to take stock of my own trajectory.

To this day when I think about Allen and what he wanted, I can't help but be saddened at how unfair and unpredictable life can be. In a truly ironic twist, I ultimately became the doctor Allen wanted to be, largely because of the Vietnam War. He, on the other hand, ended up marrying a nurse he met when he was in the Navy. He survived the war but was murdered in 2001 during a home robbery in Austin, after re-enrolling at the University of Texas to finally fulfill his dreams. When I heard about Allen's murder, all I could think was, "Shit really does happen."

But in the fall of 1968, it was obvious that I needed to check where my future was going. I was filled with concern but certain something really exciting and profitable awaited me.

When I registered for second-semester classes my sophomore year, I was assigned a math department counselor. I wasn't sure why I needed a counselor, but I thought that maybe he could help me figure out what I was going to do with my math degree, so I scheduled an appointment.

A few days later I walked across campus to the math department and my counselor's office at Batts Hall, one of the old stone buildings that make up the "six-pack" in front of the Tower. It was early morning and I was ready. Standing in front of the heavy, dark, double wooden doors, I took a deep breath and walked in. I was immediately confronted by a dim, elongated, musty hall that led into the bowels of the building. I found room 144, opened the faded wooden door, and stepped into my first taste of reality since arriving in Austin.

Directly in front of me sat my potential future: a balding man in his mid-forties with a few tufts of uncombed gray hair. He wore a faded, wrinkled, green-checked shirt. A big roll of fat hung over a belt I suspected was there but couldn't see. His office had no windows, and a single overhead light illuminated the room. His desk was covered with piles of papers, most of which were covered with a thin but perceptible layer of dust.

The scene was less than inspirational.

I sat down, and after proper introductions, I asked what I could do with my degree. I'll never forget his response. He looked at me, frowned, and matter-of-factly said, "With a degree in math, you can teach." Then I noticed his green teeth.

Damn.

I loved and respected my teachers in Graham, but *teach?* I composed myself and asked, "What else can I do?"

"Green Teeth" responded with a very long, uncomfortable silence. I didn't like that answer, either.

I was nineteen and deep into my second year of college. UT–Austin was my dream come true: I loved the Longhorns and I was having a great time. But a degree in math was becoming problematic. I needed another major, and I needed it quickly. I had always enjoyed the sciences, so I enrolled in perceptual psychology and organic chemistry. Both sounded impressively scientific, and surely they would get me started toward something better.

At the same time, the United States draft boards had initiated a lottery system to determine who was to be drafted, in what order, and when. I assumed (naively) that one's lottery number corresponded to where his birthday fell in the year, and the closer that number was to 365, the longer he stayed away from the draft and Vietnam. I wasn't too worried, because my birthday is August 25, the 237th day of the year. It all sounded fair and reasonable to me until I received my lottery number the summer before my junior year—August 25, day 237 on the calendar, had been the second number drawn. My lottery number was 2.

What really happened with the lottery was that each day of the year was written on its own piece of paper. The numbers were placed into a rotating drum and drawn out, one at a time. The order in which they were drawn determined each person's lottery number. If a person's birthday were drawn first, he would be the first to be drafted.

Lucky me! I would be second in line. Boot camp and Vietnam

awaited me immediately after graduation. My only thought: *Sheeeeiiiit!*

I would be drafted in less than two years, I thought to myself, with no choice and no chance of avoiding Vietnam. Finding a new academic interest took on even more urgency. Most important, it had to be something that continued my deferment and kept me away from a bullet in the swamps of Southeast Asia for a few more years.

I never considered myself a draft dodger, but neither did I want to get myself killed. Getting out of Graham was one thing, but Vietnam was just a little farther away than I had planned on going. After some research, I discovered that mandatory military service could be deferred if I were enrolled in a postgraduate program, including medical school.

Perfect! My interest in medicine was born from nothing more complicated than a simple fear of death. I could go back to Graham as the local doc, the hometown-boy-made-good. I'd heal the sick, do a little brain surgery, and, just maybe, avoid getting killed. Those doctor's office smells quickly became a distant memory. Allen had it right after all. All I had to do was get accepted to medical school.

But there was a problem. I wasn't the first guy to have figured this out, and the competition for medical school (and most other postgraduate schools) was extremely intense. Too much beer and poker during the past few months had hurt my grades. If I wanted a chance to get into medical school, that had to change.

Thanksgiving break came, and I headed home to my job at Johns & Fletcher. No one knew about my "new plan," so I decided to try it out on my dad. Over lunch I mentioned to him that I *might* apply for medical school. He gave me a strange look, took another draw on his ever-present cigarette, and said, "I doubt you're smart enough to get in, much less be a doctor."

That, of course, reeeeaally pissed me off, but it was the perfect motivator. When I told my mom, she just smiled. I'm sure she thought, "My son, the doctor."

It's incredible what a simple little number 2 can do to improve one's study skills. Coupled with Daddy's appraisal of my intellect, that number provided a lot of academic motivation. Maybe drinking beer and sleeping were *not* the only things one could do at midnight. The quest for grades was on.

Unfortunately, my newly discovered interest in medicine came when I was working three jobs (the jock café, dorm counselor, and weekend butcher at the local Safeway store.) I quit my weekly poker game, gave up a lot of parties, and developed a love for the UT library. There was only one year to get my grades back to medical school standards.

As fate would have it, in the middle of this bookworm phase, I met Jenny. We had enrolled in the same psychology class. Our paths had crossed in a freshman English class, but nothing came of it. This time, however, I was love-struck. Jenny was a beautiful, fun, charming girl from Greenville, another small Texas town a couple of hours from Graham. There were at least 16,000 other girls at UT, and I couldn't believe I'd missed Jenny.

She was a Gamma Phi Beta, one of the few people in her sorority I had NOT dated. I was from Graham and had no money to join a fraternity, and the Gamma Phi Beta girls threw great parties with free beer and a band. More important, the girls were not like those other, "uppity" sorority girls; they weren't embarrassed to go out with a non-Greek guy. I was in heaven, and heaven just happened to be the Gamma Phi Beta house.

By this time I was obsessed with one of two possibilities: being drafted and dying, or getting into medical school. Jenny was a special-education major with real employment opportunities in her future. I was the "whatever it takes not to get drafted" major. We started dating, went to a few football games and a few parties, but mostly we just talked. The relationship blossomed and we grew very close very quickly. A few months later I decided to propose to her.

The scene: Zilker Park, in the front seat of my secondhand, brownish-gold Corvair coupe. It was definitely not a cool Thunderbird, but it was cheap, got good gas mileage, and could go from zero to sixty in five minutes. I didn't have a ring, I didn't have a clue, but I was absolutely certain I wanted to marry Jenny, even though I wasn't sure what she saw in me.

That night, in my Corvair in Zilker Park, I was nervous. I grew very silent, took a deep breath, coughed, cleared my throat, and finally just blurted it out, "Judy, will you marry me?" As soon as the words cleared my lips, I shuddered. *Judy? Judy? Why the hell did I say Judy?*

I didn't want to marry Judy! The woman I was in love with was Jenny. Why had I said Judy? She was one of Jenny's sorority sisters I had dated for a while but hadn't seen in months.

Smooth move.

I sat there, desperately hoping Jenny was so emotionally overwhelmed that she didn't notice. Unfortunately, she was listening very carefully. Later, during my anatomy class in medical school, I learned that women just aren't built the same as men; they notice everything and remember it forever.

I remembered my dad's favorite saying: If you find yourself in a hole, the first thing to do is stop digging. But I was pretty nervous, so I just kept digging, one shovel full after another. I tried, "You're so excited, you just misunderstood me." No luck. "I didn't say that at all" didn't work, and "I didn't really say that, did I?" just upset her more. I even tried, "Who is Judy?" That one really had no chance. She kept on crying, ignoring every one of my lame excuses.

When I finally stopped talking and her tear ducts ran dry, we went to a bar. I told her I was just a little nervous, but I really loved her and wanted to marry her—she was the best thing that had ever come into my life. A couple of beers later, Jenny made me the happiest guy on the planet when she accepted.

Now my only problem was the draft/medical school issue. I had applied to all four Texas medical schools, but my scores on the General Knowledge section of the Medical College Admission Test (MCAT) were awful. I'd grown up in Graham, and the MCAT experts were asking me who painted the *Blue Boy*. I had never heard of the *Blue Boy* and really didn't care who painted it. Art history wasn't a big part of the Graham High School curriculum. There wasn't a single question on that godforsaken test about cleaning a twelve-gauge shotgun or cutting a good T-bone steak.

However, my science and math scores were good enough to give me a fighting chance, so I was invited to interview at Dallas, Galveston, and San Antonio. I was certain I could impress them one-on-one, so the planning began. When Jenny and I talked about the interviews, she asked what I was going to wear. *Wear?* I hadn't thought about that; I had figured my personality would be enough. She suggested that I should wear a suit. It was a nice idea, but I didn't own one. She soon convinced me that maybe interviewing for draft-deferring medical school while wearing blue jeans was actually *not* a good idea.

The next day I spent what little money I had saved for the Scholz beer garden on a thirty-five-dollar suit that Jenny later described as "the ugliest piece of crap [she'd] ever seen." Ever since, she has tried to teach me a little about tasteful fashion. No luck so far.

My interview in Galveston was with Truman Blocker, MD (the younger brother of Dan Blocker, of *Bonanza* and Ponderosa Ranch fame). He was chairman of plastic surgery at the University of Texas

Medical Branch at Galveston (UTMB) and, like his brother, was a gargantuan man. He bent his head forward, looking over menacing, half-lens glasses, and began the interview. He made a shark look friendly. Much later I learned that he actually was a gentle, caring giant, but I sure didn't see it that morning.

During my interview he asked me how I had been able to work so many jobs and still make my grades. He asked me about my hometown, my dad's store, dove hunting, and meat cutting. He asked why I wanted to come to medical school in Galveston and what I wanted to do with my degree. He didn't say a single word about my MCAT scores. I don't think he really cared who painted *Blue Boy* any more than I did. (So far, during my thirty years of practicing medicine, no one has asked me about *Blue Boy*, so I guess he was right.)

A few weeks after that interview, the happiest and most proud moment in my life (except for Jenny saying "yes") came. I dropped by my mailbox and found a letter from UTMB at Galveston. My heart dropped. I'd already received a really nice "we wish you luck in your future endeavors" rejection letter from Dallas and a short, terse "thanks for applying" from San Antonio (which, by the way, didn't even have a medical school yet—I had applied for the first class). So I was prepared for this letter to be more of the same. "Vietnam, here I come," I thought.

Nervously I ripped open the envelope, and the first word I saw was "Congratulations." I don't remember much after that. Forty years later, I still get a chill and almost cry when I think about reading that word, "Congratulations."

I had two weeks to accept or reject my position in the UTMB freshman class of 1970, and it took one nanosecond to decide. Jenny got the first call, and my mom and dad got the second. Daddy replied with his trademark "Hope you make it, son."

After accepting my spot in Galveston, I found out that Jenny was way ahead of me. She had applied for a teaching job in Galveston even before I asked her to marry me, and the job was hers. She figured out what was coming before I knew.

Because of what I'd learned at Johns & Fletcher, from Allen, and at UT, I was deferred from military service for the next four years. God, I was beginning to love medicine.

CHAPTER FOUR

Galveston

Jenny and I were married Saturday, August 8, 1970, in a small Methodist church in Greenville, Texas. We honeymooned in that well-known party town of Tyler, Texas, in the "honeymoon suite" at the local Holiday Inn. It really wasn't a honeymoon suite; the motel just called it that so they could charge me more. The next morning, two weeks before I started med school and Jenny began teaching, we drove through Houston and over the Galveston Causeway, directly into our future. A month prior, we'd rented Ferry Road Apartments number 91, a cheap Galveston apartment three blocks from UTMB and two blocks from the beach. Life couldn't get better than that.

Number 91 had one bedroom, a small living area, one bathroom, and a kitchen large enough for both of us to work, as long as neither one turned around or tried to open the fridge. I never understood the numbering system of Ferry Road Apartments. There were only twenty-eight apartments in the entire complex, so how could we be in number 91? Maybe the owners thought the complex would seem more elegant if they used larger numbers. The empty apartment looked absolutely huge to us when we rented it, but after a quick trip to Finger Furniture Rental, we crowded the place with cheap, ugly furniture. We were young, in love, and about as oblivious to the real world as two people could be.

The couple living directly upstairs from us had a pair of basset hounds—not great dogs for a small apartment—who bayed most every night for the first week. There were several other dogs around, so we decided to become pet owners. Junior, an eight-week-old Boston terrier mix, became our "first child." He cost five dollars. The females in the litter were too expensive; they cost seven fifty.

The first week of September, we started medical school. Medical school is a joint venture, in every sense of the term, for married couples, as challenging for the spouse as it is for the student. Med students tend to be anxious, self-centered, much too serious, and very impressed with themselves. In Jenny's case, it was her job to put up with me for four years while holding down a full-time job that supported us. Appropriately, at the end of that time, she was awarded a "Widow of Medicine" degree. It now hangs in our utility room.

Until a couple of days before my first class, I hadn't thought much about actually *attending* medical school. Securing a spot (and deferment) had been my sole priority. And after our wedding I was into being a newlywed and accepting all the praise and adulation for *planning* to be a doctor. I didn't have time to consider what would actually happen once school began. But days before my start date, old familiar doubts began to creep in. Daddy's "Hope you make it, son" began to resonate in my thoughts.

Jenny started her first day as a special-education teacher at Booker T. Washington Elementary School the same day I began medical school classes. We got up early that day, dressed, had a little breakfast, and she dropped me off at the front entrance to John Sealy Hospital. I was dressed in a short-sleeved, solid white "barber coat" with a clerical collar and a vertical row of snaps down the left side. All freshman and sophomore medical students were required to wear these. I suppose we looked a little like a cross between a priest and a barber, but I didn't care. To me the white coat just screamed DOCTOR! To everyone else it said, "Look out, here comes another dumb first-year (or second-year) student."

My first class was biochemistry. It had been one of the most difficult courses I had taken in college. I located the lecture hall, opened the door, walked in, and stood face-to-face with 165 of what I perceived to be the most intelligent-looking people I had ever seen. What the hell was I doing here? These were smart folks, and I felt like a grocery boy from Graham!

My sudden fear culminated in a good, old-fashioned cold-sweat (and near-panic) attack. I stopped, took a deep breath, walked in, and introduced myself to Albert Einstein Jr. sitting next to me. His real name was Gary, but I swear he looked like Einstein. Dad's words, "I doubt you're smart enough," echoed between my ears. After a couple of minutes, my heart rate slowed and some of my bull-headedness returned. My next thought was directed at Dad: *I'll show you, you old SOB. I can do this!*

Two hours later, still shaking a little, I walked into my second class, gross anatomy. We quickly divided into fifteen groups, four students per group. Each member of the group was referred to as a "cadaver mate." Jim, Gary, Tim, and I introduced ourselves and gathered around a stainless-steel, waist-high, eight-foot-long box that looked to be about four feet deep. Vertical, double steel doors concealed and protected its contents.

Wide-eyed, we looked at each other, held our collective breaths, and cracked open the container an inch or so. An acidic, foul odor assaulted our nostrils. Even the warm rotten eggs I occasionally encountered at Johns & Fletcher couldn't compete with this odor.

Our eyes watered while we took very shallow breaths and tried not to gag.

This wasn't going to be easy.

Once we were able to breathe, we laughed, tried to ignore the burning in our lungs, and opened the container. There, wrapped from head to toe in a thick layer of brown-stained, formaldehyde-soaked cheesecloth lay our new best friend.

A copy of his death certificate was taped on the outside of the right door, just under the handle. It read, "Suicide from self-inflicted gunshot wound." He was thirty-eight. Stunned, I glanced at my group and knew from their faces that they were, too.

We all had the same questions: Why did he do it? What had his life been like? What on earth drove him to point a gun at himself and shoot? We were a bit overwhelmed, but when a guy in the group next to us threw up all over his cadaver and one of his cadaver mates, our mood finally lightened a bit.

Every group gave its cadaver a nickname. Using their real names made the entire experience just too creepy, so we named ours "Dick," for no particular reason. For the next six months, we spent four hours a day, five days a week with Dick.

Later, while opening his skull during the neurologic anatomy segment, we found three separate bullet holes in his skull, two on the right side and one just above his ear on the left. It would be pretty difficult to shoot oneself three times in the head, so we decided his "suicide" was a little questionable. It didn't matter much, though. Dick was ours for the next few months.

The combination of formaldehyde and death made the lab smell like hell, but we learned to cope. Usually that required a little macabre humor. One group sent out a Christmas card that year. It was a photo of five guys, standing, smiling, arms around one another's shoulders, with a nice caption wishing everyone a Merry

Christmas. Pretty touching, except that the middle guy was their cadaver. They really had a hard time getting a smile on his face for that picture.

Meanwhile, Jenny was teaching special-education students—a euphemism for kids no other teachers wanted in their classrooms. In Jenny's case, teaching meant she was a friend, caregiver, and warden to kids ages six to eighteen. At the beginning of her third month, six-year-old Talmage came in one morning, crying uncontrollably. Jenny asked why. He looked at her with teary eyes and said, "Momma got shot last night." He had no one left at home, so he just came to school. Another typical day for her.

Shortly after her arrival, she had to have a little conversation with a student in the boys' bathroom. One of the younger kids was peeing his pants, and when she asked why, he told her that an older boy was bullying him in the restroom. Jenny marched into the bathroom and up to the urinal where the bully was, looked him in the eye, told him to stop picking on little Devan, turned around, and walked out. The bully never bothered Devan again, but he did tell his buddies that that "white teacher" was crazy.

Jenny stayed at Booker T. Washington for two years, and that was two years longer than anyone thought she would make it. They just didn't know Jenny. Then she was offered an opportunity to teach at the Shriners burn hospital, one of the premier children's burn centers in the world. It was located on the UTMB campus and admitted only the most severely burned children, regardless of their ability to pay. It was a great opportunity with better pay, so she reluctantly left "her kids" at Booker T. and went to Shriners.

In one weekend she transitioned from helping her Booker T. kids survive in incredibly difficult family and social circumstances to working with severely burned children experiencing the worst life had to offer. In reality, she went from one hellhole to another, but she approached both with care and compassion that I have not seen in thirty years of practicing medicine. She taught me more about empathy than any medical school classroom ever could.

While Jenny tended to her students at Shriners, I survived gross anatomy, "Dick," and all my other classroom experiences.

At the beginning of my third year, I actually had the opportunity to interact with live patients. That required a change of coats; barber coats meant "absolutely no patient contact." The smell of formaldehyde and death never came out of the barber coat, so it went in the trash. Third- and fourth-year students wore *real* doctors' coats. They were white, poorly tailored, waist-length, and long-sleeved, and they looked like sport coats with two big pockets on either side of the center buttons. The big pockets were necessary for our "peripheral brains," the mounds of notes we carried around that summarized everything we had been taught during the past two years. It took me months to figure out that my notes were pretty worthless. By the time I sorted through them for an answer, my patient could be dead.

With my new coat, I could walk around the hospital, feel important, and actually write orders on patients' charts, even though the nurses knew to ignore anything a third-year student wrote. Yet when I began to work with people instead of books, my passion for medicine came alive.

During my third year I was introduced to the female pelvic examination, and it's an experience I'll never forget. By the time I began my three-month OB-GYN rotation, I'd seen only a few female pelvises, and none had been in medical situations. I had read the textbook chapter on pelvic exams but could not imagine what I would do when confronted with a woman in a gynecology exam room. She would expect me to figure out what was wrong and help.

How in the world would I learn to do that, much less *ever* become comfortable with it?

Our nurse instructor had the answer. Twenty-four students were on the rotation, and she divided us into groups of four. Six exam tables were arranged in a circle, the foot of each facing toward the center. A semitransparent curtain hung between each pair of tables, but nothing covered the ends.

The short, middle-aged, angry nurse stood in the center, hands on hips. She instructed the first six of us to strip from the waist down. We were told to lie on the exam tables, heels in the stirrups and legs apart. She put on a glove and did a rectal exam on each of us, one at a time, changing her glove each time, with the rest of the group watching.

We put our pants back on, KY jelly still between our cheeks, and the next group followed. When she finished, she grinned and said, "Now you know how your female patients will feel." The instruction continued with female volunteers in private exam rooms. In thirty seconds, she had taught me everything I needed to know about the *art* of performing a pelvic examination in a caring, thoughtful manner.

At the start of our senior year, every student had to decide which field of medicine he would pursue. Most of my classmates were struggling with their decision. There were so many possibilities, in radically different specialties such as internal medicine, radiology, surgery, and pediatrics, but most of us had very little experience on which to make those decisions. I was fortunate. I had already decided on family practice. I wanted to go back to Graham, be the hometown-boy-made-good, and heal the sick, every one of them.

In 1973, one of the premier family practice residency programs in the U.S. was at John Peter Smith Hospital, a county hospital in Fort Worth, Texas. Residents in that program learned to do everything from brain surgery to pediatrics. Young docs think they can do it all, and I was no exception. I applied to John Peter Smith my senior year and was a match there. In June 1974, Jenny and I left Galveston and headed to Fort Worth. Unfortunately, the rental furniture had to go with us. Junior had chewed the legs off every piece, forcing us to pay for all of it. He was a bad dog.

CHAPTER FIVE

1974: Residency

Fort Worth, Texas, Where the West Begins

Jenny, Junior, and I left Galveston in a U-Haul bobtail truck loaded with our chewed-up, newly financed furniture. We were pretty emotional as we watched Galveston Island disappear behind the causeway, but the nostalgia passed quickly. Jenny had secured a job teaching homebound students, mostly pregnant teenagers who weren't allowed to attend regular classes in Fort Worth, and I was a first-year doctor, interning in family practice.

Two days later, we were signing a lease for our new Fort Worth apartment. I was bubbly. "We" had graduated from medical school, and signing the lease would be my first chance to write "Alan Johns, MD" on an official document. Our new landlord, a grumpy guy wearing a plaid work shirt and jeans, gummed a half-smoked cigarette and grinned as he pushed the lease to my side of the table and said, "Sign here," pointing toward the bottom of the page. I mumbled something back and wrote "Alan Johns, MD" in large, clear cursive on the signature line. I sat back, grinned, and felt my shirt buttons tighten as my chest puffed out. Damn, it felt good to write that. I waited for "Grumpy" to be impressed. Much to my dismay, he didn't even comment about the fact that I was a doctor. All he cared about was a check that wasn't going to bounce. When we left, Jenny laughed and said maybe, just maybe, I was a little too impressed with myself. A day later we moved in, and Junior went right back to chewing his favorite kitchen table leg.

In 1974 a family practice residency required three years of training, and obstetrics and gynecology required four. Both started with what was called a "rotating internship." That simply meant spending from one to three months immersed in each of the major specialties—internal medicine, pediatrics, surgery, orthopedics, and OB-GYN.

Ten of us started at John Peter Smith Hospital on July 1, 1974. Two interns were rotating in OB-GYN, and the rest of us were in family practice. We were all bursting with newly acquired knowledge, energy, enthusiasm, and confidence. We were a bunch of green interns about to learn a lot of hard lessons.

My first day as a "real" doctor began at 8:00 a.m. in the pediatric outpatient clinic. Blissfully oblivious and full of bravado, I strutted in wearing my new, freshly ironed, brilliant-white "real doctor" coat. A prescription pad was stuffed in the right pocket, each page eagerly awaiting my signature. I introduced myself to the nurses and was struck by their strange, almost comedic attitudes. They even seemed to snicker a little as they said, "Good morning, *Doctor* Johns." Most had been working in the pediatric clinic for years and had been through this July 1 "coming-out" ritual many times.

One of the nurses handed me a chart, and I studied it for a minute or so. "Do you want me to go into the exam room with you?" she asked. Inside the chart, the handwritten notes of my predecessor were indecipherable, but I wasn't about to let on.

I closed the chart, gave her my best serious-doctor expression, and said, "No thanks, I can handle it." She just smiled and said, "Call if you need me."

Taking a deep breath, I walked down the hall to exam room three, opened the door, and walked directly into a three-foot stream of yellow vomit being expelled by a two-year-old boy in the arms of his distraught, sleep-deprived mother. The vomit engulfed the front of my brand-new coat, leaving a few Cheerio chunks clinging to the buttons.

Only then did it hit me: This kid was human. I was about to write a prescription that could actually be filled. Reading about a sick child in a pediatrics textbook was one thing, but being responsible for diagnosing and treating one was totally different. Plus the kid in front of me didn't look like the pictures in the book. He was little and sick and needed my help, and I still saw myself as the guy from Graham who didn't know who painted *Blue Boy*. And now I had vomit all over my coat.

With my confidence a little shaken, I excused myself and stepped into the hallway to look for a wet towel. The pediatric nurses had been joined by the family practice resident, who had just completed his intern year. They were all laughing uncontrollably. Then the head nurse held up a handwritten sign: "Welcome to Pediatrics, Dr. Johns." My initiation was complete, as far as the staff was concerned.

Two months later, all the kids I had treated during my pediatric rotation survived, but the experience reminded me of the crying, sick, smelly kids I'd encountered in the doctor's office in Graham. When my two months ended, I also was convinced that most of the civilized world had been overrun by kids with snotty noses and diarrhea running out the sides of their diapers, down their legs, and onto my lap.

I was more than ready to try something else.

That something else was my next rotation: internal medicine, the adult version of pediatrics. Internal medicine docs spend all day treating nondescript aches and pains, high blood pressure, obesity, diabetes, headaches, bellyaches, coughs, sore throats, depression, and other equally unexciting (at least to me) infirmities. And on top of that, infected patients expose their internists (and pediatricians) to new and vicious strains of viruses on a daily basis, making the doctors a cesspool of infectious disease and perpetually as sick as the patients they treat.

I spent the next four months near death, continuously coughing up yellow stuff, my nose running like Niagara Falls and my sinuses stopped up tighter than a Baptist's whiskey bottle. I'm sure that during those four months I contracted every viral illness known to science, and quite probably a few new ones.

Yet I learned a lot about being a doctor from this rotation. Ninety percent of my patients were pleasant elderly ladies, and for them the medical clinic was a social outing. They always arrived dressed up, carrying walking canes and sacks stuffed with their medicines. They'd dump what seemed to be about a hundred prescription bottles on my desk, then ignore them to catch me up on their life stories. They didn't seem to care much about diagnoses or treatment; they just needed to talk to someone. It was much later in the visit before they worried about getting their prescriptions filled. I'm sure they repeated the same routine at their local pharmacy.

During those four months, I did a lot of listening and writing. It wasn't until much later that I realized those ladies taught me something that never appears in any medical school curriculum. In medical school, students are taught to ask the "right questions" that "target" particular organ systems so they can arrive at the proper diagnosis. During this rotation, however, I learned that good medicine is also about listening, not talking. If doctors are good listeners, their patients will almost always tell them exactly what is wrong. To this day, "listening and nodding" have served me well.

During this same time, I noticed that I rarely saw old men, and that struck me as strange. One of the senior medical residents explained the phenomenon this way: All the old men were either dead or had no desire to go to the doctor unless they were on a stretcher. We only saw them in the ER when something was *really* wrong.

By the end of my internal medicine rotation, I had signed "Alan Johns, MD" so many damn times that my signature vaguely resembled a cursive "A" followed by a squiggly line and some indecipherable letters. The thrill of writing "MD" was gone, and a lifetime of "doctor's handwriting" was emerging.

Moonlighting

My resident's salary provided little more than beer money, and most interns moonlighted to supplement our income. "Moonlighting" is an appropriate term because the extra work always started after sunset on Friday and ended early Monday morning. Not surprisingly, that's exactly the length of time most private-practice doctors require to recover from a week in their offices.

Small, rural emergency rooms used moonlighting interns to fill in on weekends, freeing the local docs from that responsibility. And as luck would have it, in early October, Jimmy J., one of the family docs in Graham, called and offered me an opportunity to cover the Graham Emergency Room on weekends. I was ecstatic. Only a few months out of medical school, I would be living out my "hometown-boy-made-good" dream, even if it were only on weekends. I jumped at the chance, having no clue that the decision would change my life.

My first weekend came, and after the ninety-mile drive, I arrived at the Graham hospital at 6:00 p.m. on a cool, cloudy Friday evening in November. The small emergency room was at the back of the hospital, its double doors opening onto a minuscule asphalt parking lot that was big enough for an ambulance and a couple of cars. Inside and immediately adjacent to the ER was my new weekend home: a sleep room with a small pullout bed, a phone, and a TV. A cookie jar sat on a desk at the end of the couch/bed, adjacent to the telephone. Every morning it was filled with warm, freshly baked chocolate chip cookies.

After I settled in, the ladies from the hospital kitchen came by to introduce themselves and explained they would bring me a home-cooked breakfast, lunch, and dinner every day. Eureka, another job involving free food!

What I didn't realize was that the sleepy Graham Hospital emergency room awakened with a vengeance on the weekends. Graham was dry (no alcohol sales within the city limits), so everyone teetotaled—until Friday night, when all hell broke loose.

The Corral, a bar/liquor store/nightclub, was located just fifteen minutes northeast of town, a legal twenty yards beyond the city limits. Possum Kingdom Lake lay a scant ten minutes farther. At least half the teenagers in town, as well as quite a few adults, visited one or both every summer weekend.

The combination of liquor and lake kept the ER busy from midnight Friday until the last drunk staggered out around noon Saturday. Then the patient lineup started all over again Saturday night. Most Saturday evening clients were sewn up, sober, and ready for morning church services by 11:00 a.m. Sunday. I ended up treating hundreds of cuts, bruises, broken bones, and black eyes from minor disagreements at the Corral and "misfortunes" at Possum Kingdom.

During my second weekend working in this frenzy, I had an epiphany. I had just completed two months of pediatrics and the first two months of my internal medicine rotation. These two specialties constituted at least 80 percent of a family doc's business. Based on my *vast* experience, doubts about my career choice had already begun to emerge, and that Saturday night sealed the deal. I had been particularly busy between 3:00 p.m. and 1:00 a.m. sewing up lacerations, treating a flu outbreak, admitting one heart attack patient, transferring a car wreck victim to Fort Worth, and sewing up a couple of drunks suffering from an encounter with broken beer bottles. I really needed some sleep before the 3:00 a.m. "last call" onslaught began. I stumbled into the sleep room, ate a cookie, turned off the light, lay down, and pulled a sheet over my head.

Tantalizingly close to full-blown sleep, I was startled awake when the phone rang. I knew it wasn't from the ER; a nurse always knocked on my door when they needed me.

"Hello, this is Dr. Johns," I growled into the hand piece.

"Alan!" an exuberant, loud voice boomed. "Alan!"

"Yeah," I replied sleepily.

"It's Dan!" the voice said.

Dan was a classmate of mine in high school and a longtime friend who had moved back to Graham with his family. By now I was fully awake but still exhausted.

"You know, if anyone else had been at the hospital I wouldn't have called, but I knew you wouldn't mind," he said.

Since I'd just gone through my elderly-ladies-listening training, I didn't say anything, but I knew this call was trouble.

"I've had this itch in my groin for a couple of weeks, and I thought you might call in something for me," Dan said.

My mouth dropped open, but nothing came out; my vocal cords were temporarily paralyzed, unable to cope with the air rushing out of my lungs. But my brain was fully engaged.

All I could think was, *It's damned one-thirty in the morning, you moron. You've been itching for two weeks! Just what the hell do you want me to do about it in the middle of the night?*

I regained my composure as my brain quieted, and my voice returned. Turning off what I was really thinking, I calmly told Dan that he would have to be examined to figure out what was wrong, and that I had yet to go through my dermatology rotation, so I couldn't help much. He needed to call his family doctor in the morning, after the sun peeked over the horizon.

He thanked me and hung up.

I lay back down and for the first time began to seriously examine my career plan. I was less than enthused with my first two rotations. I knew almost everyone in Graham, and they knew me. It became uncomfortably obvious that, if I moved to Graham to practice medicine, Dan's call would begin a bombardment of similar calls lasting my entire career—friends and acquaintances calling me at all hours of the day and night. I'd have nowhere to hide, nor time to relax. It began to sound like a doctor's nightmare.

I finished out the weekend, drove back to Fort Worth at daybreak Monday morning, and called Jimmy, a family practitioner in Graham who'd been there for seventeen years. Loved and adored by everyone, he had taken care of my grandmother for the last fifteen years of her life. He made house calls and was often paid with peach preserves, cookies, and pies. He was an embodiment of the quintessential small-town family doctor.

Jimmy answered the phone in a good mood. For the next five minutes I spilled out my feelings and concerns. When I finished, he laughed. "Tell you a secret," he said. "No one knows, but I'm leaving Graham in eight months to do a surgery residency in Oklahoma. My wife and I simply can't take this life anymore. We love the people, but we're dying here." He was forty-five—damned old to start one of the most rigorous surgical training programs in the country, much less move his family, but he needed out of the pressures of his practice in Graham.

After talking with Jimmy, I felt better. I wasn't abandoning Graham; my dreams were just taking another course.

A few days later I began my three-month obstetrics and gynecology rotation. By the end of the first week, I'd delivered eight babies, assisted in two Cesarean sections, watched a hysterectomy, and seen my first case of gonorrhea. I loved the surgery aspect of this rotation and found that my personality was more suited to surgery than diagnostics.

The cognitive aspect of internal medicine and pediatrics was critically important to my training, but they didn't appeal to me as much as "doing stuff" with my hands. I'm aggressive, hardheaded, realistic, and detail-oriented. Once my mind is made up, I tend to get it done, and in this rotation I was having more fun than the law should allow. I found the hands-on aspect interesting, challenging, and satisfying. Most importantly, however, obstetrics was a happy specialty. Following a patient through labor and delivery had been one of the most satisfying experiences in my short medical career. Even better, I could deliver the baby and hand it off to the pediatrics intern. They could be the ones who had to dodge the streams of vomit and diarrhea. It just didn't get any better than that.

I talked with Jenny about switching out of family practice. She was all for the change, because she hadn't been particularly enthusiastic about moving to Graham. When my surgery rotation started, I talked with Dr. Staples, the chief of OB-GYN, about changing residencies. Two months of general surgery further confirmed my suspicions; I really loved the challenge and pressure of surgery and the joy of obstetrics.

Finally I'd found my niche. It didn't take long for that niche to become my passion.

CHAPTER SIX

OB-GYN

The switch from a family practice residency to OB-GYN offered a challenge: Every OB-GYN position in the John Peter Smith Hospital program was filled. Fortunately, the hospital was growing rapidly, and Dr. Staples had applied for an additional residency slot. But the position had not yet been approved. My only option was to locate a residency with a second-year vacancy at another hospital. I called twenty programs and found only two openings. Getting into an OB-GYN residency didn't look promising.

I was also dealing with an issue that ultimately would turn out to be an asset more than a liability. I was born with strabismus, known as lazy eye or cross-eye. Usually diagnosed by age two, the condition is characterized by an imbalance of the extra-ocular muscles that move the eyeballs; they are not synchronized and don't focus on the same thing simultaneously. When this happens to a child (up to about age seven), the part of the brain that controls vision, the optic hemisphere, blocks out the image from one eye (even though the eye works fine). When adults develop this problem (sometimes from an injury to the eye sockets), they usually develop uncorrectable double vision.

After my condition was diagnosed, my ophthalmologic surgeon shortened and lengthened some of my six extra-ocular muscles during five surgeries in four years. My parents hoped that the surgeon would get both of my eyes to point at the same thing simultaneously. But none of the surgeries worked. If this "muscle imbalance" can't be corrected by age seven, the brain permanently blocks out the image from one eye forever, and that's what happened to me. I have perfect vision in my left eye and am legally blind in my right. My right eye works fine; my brain just doesn't see the image it transmits.

I had done fine all my life with this condition, except for my lack of depth perception, which becomes very important when objects are more than a few feet away. When an object is close, we use other senses, specifically touch and proprioception (our sense of where the various parts of our bodies are in relation to one another), to create a three-dimensional picture of our surroundings, which makes binocular depth perception less important. Fortunately, my ocular muscle imbalance was not a hindrance to becoming an OB-GYN specialist, because patients in surgery are lying only a few inches away. I would simply be a one-eyed surgeon.

When the new OB-GYN slot at John Peter Smith still hadn't been approved after a few months, I interviewed for the two vacant, second-year residency spots while Dr. Staples waited for the Residency Review Committee to make up its mind about his third position. To my delight, the committee approved Dr. Staples' application, and I secured the new slot. My family medicine career officially ended on July 1, 1975, when I became a second-year OB-GYN resident at John Peter Smith.

Instantly my medical education was transformed from daily drudgery to long days filled with the most interesting and fulfilling challenges I could imagine. Despite fourteen- to eighteen-hour workdays, I was like a kid whose four grandparents, vying for his attention, had taken him to a toy store.

In family practice residency, the joke was that family practice docs had to "learn less and less about more and more until they knew nothing about everything." The specialists, of course, "learned more and more about less and less until they knew everything about nothing." There is a bit of truth in both.

The ability to focus entirely on one area was refreshing. I was instantly intrigued, and my eagerness to progress was insatiable. I wanted to be in the operating room for every surgery and every delivery, day or night, no matter how tired I was. Unfortunately, third- and fourth-year residents outranked me, so I was relegated to watching a lot and *assigned* to draw blood, start IVs, change bandages, complete physical exams, and give enemas to laboring patients. All of this was a necessary initiation a resident must go through while slowly learning the good stuff.

I did get to sew a little, however. The senior-level residents always performed surgery with the attending staff while the second-year residents dutifully stood beside the operating table in full operating room regalia, far from the blood. However, after a procedure was completed, someone had to sew up the incision. Since that's the least interesting facet of surgery, it always fell to the "low man." As second-year residents, we took on the task with the intensity of plastic surgeons. Every incision was closed with meticulous precision, and we admired our work every bit as much as Michelangelo must have.

About midyear I scrubbed, gowned, gloved, and walked into the operating room expecting another observe-only experience. The patient was a slender young woman who'd been admitted for a hysterectomy. Her abdomen had been prepped and the surgical drapes were in place. Our scrub nurse, the senior resident, and Dr.

Staples were crowded around the two-foot by two-foot opening in the drapes that exposed her flat abdomen from the belly button to the pubic bone. Her skin had taken on an orange hue from the Betadine used to sterilize it in preparation for the procedure. I nervously inched closer to the operating table, hoping for a better vantage point, when Dr. Staples suddenly turned around, looked me straight in the eye (fortunately, my good one,) handed me the scalpel, stepped back, and said, "Here, you start."

I swear my heart stopped. Wow! My chance had come! Emboldened, I took the knife, stepped up to the operating table, looked down at that pristine abdomen, and damn near threw up. My problem: I had NEVER cut anyone open. I had sewn up quite a few but never actually cut one. Quickly composing myself, I moved the scalpel down toward her orange-tinted skin, took a breath, readied myself, and thought, *Where the hell do I cut?*

I'd watched hundreds of surgeries, but I'd never really thought about how to start. How long and deep should the incision be? Crap. Once I started, I couldn't take back the opening I'd made if it were in the wrong place.

Trying to calm myself, I touched her skin with the blade in an area I thought might be okay. Holding my breath, I pushed down, moving the scalpel across her lower abdomen. To my surprise, my effort only scratched the skin. Embarrassed, I tried again. Nothing. By now I was sweating profusely and hyperventilating, but out of the corner of my eye I noticed that everyone in the operating room was laughing uncontrollably.

What the hell was wrong?

Dr. Staples' eyes squinted as he grinned beneath his mask. He calmly reached over, took the scalpel, turned it over, and handed it back. Now the sharp side was down. He cleared his throat and said, "Try again—it cuts better this way."

With that somewhat shaky start, my surgical career began in earnest.

Early in my third year, a new surgical procedure called laparoscopy, or "belly-button surgery," was being developed. It was the beginning of what was to become "minimally invasive surgery." During laparoscopic surgery, carbon dioxide is used to inflate the abdomen like a balloon, then a hole is cut in the umbilicus (belly button) and a telescope-like instrument called a laparoscope is threaded through the hole. Light is directed through the scope, and the surgeon can look inside the abdomen without making a big incision. This procedure was very revolutionary at the time, and the next logical step was to actually operate through the small incisions instead of just looking inside.

In my world, laparoscopy was easy; I was used to seeing out of only one eye, and that's what the laparoscope required. However, laparoscopy was particularly difficult for surgeons with normal, binocular vision, because they depended on their two eyes for depth perception. Because laparoscopy came naturally to me, I had a front-row seat to this new technology, which was destined to transform the operating room.

A medical emergency very close to home interrupted my third year of residency: My dad was admitted to Harris Methodist Hospital in Fort Worth for removal of a cancerous tumor in his colon. He had a horrible case of emphysema from smoking most of his life. After nearly three years of residency, I had learned just enough to understand that Daddy might not survive the surgery, because operating on a patient with severe emphysema is a disaster waiting to happen.

My mom and sister were scared enough about the cancer, so I didn't discuss my fears about his emphysema and the complications it might bring. They had enough to worry about. During his surgery, we sat in the waiting room for what seemed like hours, my apprehension growing by the minute. Suddenly, a chubby nurse dressed in scrubs strolled out of the recovery room looking for the Johns family. In a serious, businesslike tone, she told us that Daddy had suffered a cardiac arrest on the operating table but had been resuscitated. Before any of us could get a word out, she disappeared through the door.

Eyes full of tears, my mom and sister looked toward me—the doctor—for reassurance. I had none, so we sat again and continued waiting. A few minutes later, Daddy's surgeon came into the waiting room. He was in scrubs with his surgical cap still covering his hair. His mask was untied, hanging around his neck with a few speckles of blood on the front. He wore his knee-length doctor's coat with his name monogrammed above the left pocket, and he projected a rather impressive but imposing and arrogant attitude.

Tearing off his surgical cap, he looked at us and said, "We did what we had to do." With that, he walked away, with no other explanation! We wanted to ask questions about the tumor, the surgery outcome, the complications, recovery, and prognosis, but the doctor had disappeared. I was so stunned and angry, I couldn't speak, and my mind was racing. I wanted to run after the surgeon and say, "Of course, you arrogant prick. I assume you did what you had to do—that's what doctors do." But I held back, and we were left with only the fact that Daddy was alive.

Daddy survived, but the surgeon's arrogance still angers me. It did, though, forever influence the way I interact with my patients and their family members. Ever since that day, when I finish a surgical case, I sit with the family and answer every question, no matter how long it takes and no matter how busy I am. I never want my patients' families to feel like my family felt after Dad's surgery because I was too busy or aloof to talk with them.

I didn't realize it, but my long journey from being a technician to becoming a physician, in the truest sense of the word, began on that day.

I spent my fourth and last year of residency working as hard as I had ever worked. At John Peter Smith the senior residents were in charge of overseeing the first-, second-, and third-year residents as they performed their duties in the outpatient clinics, operating rooms, delivery rooms, and emergency room. Although our faculty physicians were ultimately responsible, this was our one chance to spread our wings and learn to fly solo before going out on our own. Partly because of all this responsibility and partly because of my youth, I felt pretty cocky and bulletproof, much like the other fourth-year residents did. Midway through the year, I was pretty convinced that the my experiences the prior three and a half years had taught me most everything I needed to know.

That all changed about 1:00 a.m. one bitterly cold January night. I was the senior resident in charge when I was paged to the emergency room. Unless it was a life-threatening emergency, the interns, second-year, and third-year residents handled everything. They performed the initial evaluations of all patients, then reported to the senior resident, and that night it was me. If I couldn't take care of the situation or had questions, I called the faculty physician at home. By this time, however, I was pretty certain I could handle just about anything that came my way.

After getting the call, I strolled into the ER and was directed to bed number three by one of the nurses. The ER had twenty-four beds, separated by dull yellow curtains that hung from the ceiling. I pulled back the curtain and was confronted with more blood than I'd ever seen. A woman in her early twenties lay there, pale as skim milk and with terror-filled eyes, panting as if she'd just run a sprint.

I yelled for a nurse, then pulled back the sheet. A huge, bloody mass protruded from between her legs. She had told no one about being pregnant and had delivered her baby at home. The infant was fine, but when the woman had tried to pull out the placenta, her uterus everted—turned inside out—and protruded outward. When this happens, the uterus can't contract and thus can't stop bleeding, and massive hemorrhage ensues. The woman had barely made it to the phone to call an ambulance.

Although I had heard of uterine eversion, I had no experience with it. The woman had no blood pressure, a weak pulse, extremely rapid respiration, and eyes that were crying out, "Help me, please."

In the next twenty minutes, we started IVs, gave her every pint of matching blood we could find, and worked feverishly to get the uterus back in place, all in an attempt to get her stable enough to move her into the OR, where a definitive procedure could be done. Her heart stopped, and we resuscitated her, several times.

Despite all we did, she died on that blood-soaked bed in front of me. To this day I can envision the helpless, pleading expression in her eyes.

After she died, I pulled back the curtain and walked away, completely devastated and crying uncontrollably. I had trained day and night for the past three and a half years for exactly this situation, and I'd failed.

I changed scrubs, sat down, and tried to grasp what had happened. All my training, work, studying, and experience meant nothing. I wasn't bulletproof, nor was I the doc with all the answers. I had done everything I had been trained to do and still failed. The rest of the night seemed to take months to pass, and daylight didn't bring much relief.

In hindsight I realize that the experience taught me the most valuable lesson a physician—particularly a young, confident one— can learn: Medicine would be a lifelong learning experience. My training had equipped me with the basics, but what I *didn't* know was suddenly overwhelming and incomprehensible.

After four years of residency and hundreds of weekends in small-town ERs, my confidence had reached a peak, and I'd been programmed to act instead of think when faced with a crisis. Doctors can't take too much time to think in an emergency situation—we must act, and act quickly. The learning part has to come before the emergency happens.

My confidence had been shattered that night, and I began to question what I knew. How capable was I? After many days and sleepless nights, I realized just how much I still had to learn. As the years went on, I also realized that, because medicine progresses and changes every day, my dedication to the profession had to be total and complete to keep up. Now every time I get bored listening to an expert's lecture or think I really don't need to attend an educational program, I flash back to the young woman's eyes on that cold January night.

The morning after her death, I made the commitment to every future patient that I would never stop trying to be the best doctor I could be. I couldn't help everyone in every situation, but it wouldn't be because I hadn't worked hard enough.

I also realized that not everyone can be saved, not even all young, healthy women. But medicine forces me to push back that reality and practice as if it were not true. That's quite a conundrum for any physician! But we learn to deal with it.

Many people over the years have asked me if I believe in medical miracles. I never answer. After that January night, I began believing in the skilled, dedicated, selfless folks who make the fruit of their work seem like miracles.

· · ·

Also during my fourth year of residency, Jenny and I had our first child, Julie. Including Junior, our furniture-chewing dog, we became a family of four. I didn't yet have a job lined up, and I figured it was about time. After eleven years of education, I needed to make a living and apply what I'd learned. The time had finally come to grow roots and settle down. Jenny and I loved Fort Worth. It was ideally located, equidistant between Graham and Greenville, so we decided that Fort Worth would be our permanent home.

Six months before I finished my residency, another fourth-year resident named Larry and I decided to open an OB-GYN practice on the north side of Fort Worth. We found an empty veterinary office that had been a Pizza Hut a few years before. We borrowed the money to renovate it into a medical office and planned to open for business on July 1, 1977, the day after we were to finish our residency.

As usual, I figured my life was set. But in late May, after a long night on call and while encouraging my last patient to push out her fifth child, another life-altering event happened.

"Dr. Johns, call the operator," a voice requested over the hospital loudspeaker. Doctors hear these pages all the time. Usually they are meant to alert us about a new admission, which also means there's more work to do. I answered the call hesitantly.

David, an OB-GYN doctor who had supervised one of my rotations earlier in the year, was on the phone. He was in his mid-forties and had a very busy practice at the Catholic hospital adjacent to John Peter Smith.

"Hey, Alan," he said. Hearing his voice, I wondered what was up. "Want to buy my practice?" Never one for small talk, he had gotten right to the point.

Since starting my medical career, I had been speechless only three times: when Dan wanted something for his itch, with Daddy's surgeon, and now, when David offered his thriving practice. I finally managed, "How much do you want?"

"Just the depreciated value of the furniture and equipment, about eight thousand dollars."

I was stunned. Before I could ask any other questions, he said, "Let me know tomorrow," then hung up.

I went back to work, and my patient pushed out her third boy, whom I caught and passed off to the pediatric resident. A nanosecond later I called my new partner, Larry, and told him about the deal. We decided to accept David's offer. It was simply too good to pass up.

Eighteen hours later we added eight thousand dollars to our debt and wrote David a check. He moved out of town later that week, leaving a booming practice and a full office staff. Larry and I wondered why David was in such a rush to leave, but we didn't ask. We were simply too busy getting ready for our new venture to worry about that little detail. A few years later we were told that David needed to get out of town quickly to stay just in front of some folks from Las Vegas to whom he owed "a little money."

So there we were. Larry and I were three weeks from finishing our residency and found ourselves proud owners of two offices and a busy OB-GYN practice that we had no idea how to manage. On my first day in David's old office, I introduced myself to a dozen obstetrical patients (some due in a few weeks), two patients already scheduled for surgery, and an office staff wondering what the hell was happening.

Even with all the pressure, I fell in love with the routine. Normally it takes at least three years for a new doctor to build a practice. My fortunate combination of luck and timing allowed me to start mine with a full slate of patients, no practice-building necessary.

In addition, my knack for laparoscopy and a waiting room full of patients were a perfect combination, one that allowed me to develop the expertise in laparoscopic surgery that was to define my career.

My practice rapidly grew, and a scant six years later I had developed sufficient experience and expertise in laparoscopic surgery to begin teaching it. Despite my misgivings in college about teaching math, I found instructing surgery to be more professionally fulfilling than most anything I had ever done.

At this same time, the drive my dad instilled in me was at full throttle, and I began traveling, lecturing, and writing medical articles, all the while maintaining a very busy surgical practice. The time I spent with my family was dwindling, but I always figured I could catch up later.

It took only a few years for me to accumulate more than ten thousand hours in the operating room. According to research quoted in Malcolm Gladwell's nonfiction best seller *Outliers*, becoming an "expert" in most any profession requires ten thousand hours of practice. In my little corner of the gynecological world, I was known as one of its experts.

I also developed an interest in in vitro fertilization (test-tube babies), ultrasound, and clinical research. My career blossomed and my confidence boomed. I was a lucky man. It never occurred to me that anything in my life could go wrong. In short, I became pretty full of myself.

In 1982, we had added another baby girl—Jessica—to our brood and had bought a beautiful home in Fort Worth. Jenny and I were experiencing life at its fullest.

A mere ten years later, the unthinkable happened.

CHAPTER SEVEN

March 7, 1998

Long before I got the call from Fred, the pathologist who informed me of my diagnosis, I'd discovered the problem myself. I still get nervous thinking about the evening I faced the mirror and realized I might be in trouble.

In 1988, ten years before I discovered the lump, I'd taken up golf, and I really loved the game. I was never much of an athlete in school, but I did enjoy outdoor activities, and golf offered the perfect combination of fresh air, exercise, challenges, and friends.

Alas, my enthusiasm never translated into skill, but I had a great time playing. I golfed most weekends when I wasn't traveling and teaching.

On March 7, 1998, I went out early for my normal Saturday game. The day was beautiful: sixty-five degrees, blue skies, and no wind. I walked the golf course, and on the fifteenth hole, I remember stopping to look up at the vast, cloudless sky and thinking how fortunate I was.

I finished the round, carrying my clubs and hitting the damnable little ball more times than I care to remember. By the time it was over, I was sweaty and tired, but satisfied. I headed home, rushed through the front door, said hello to Jenny and the kids, and went straight for the shower. Jenny and I were due to leave for a dinner dance and auction benefiting my daughter Jessica's school that night, and my tux was laid out on the bed. I was looking forward to a fun evening sitting with three other couples who also had kids in Jessica's class.

After showering, I grabbed a towel, wrapped it around my waist, and glanced in the mirror to check for love handles. Right after Julie was born, I had blimped out to 240 pounds and really didn't like what I saw in the mirror very much. So I dieted and exercised for a year and got back to 170. After all that work, I was determined never to gain the weight back, and I'd become a little vain about the matter.

There were no love handles, but what I did see in that mirror made my blood run cold. I drew in a sharp, deep breath. My right nipple was inverted. The left one was perfectly normal, poking outward, but the right one was sucked in. I blinked a couple of times and leaned closer to the mirror, certain I was wrong.

But I wasn't.

Cold drops of sweat beaded under my arms and across my forehead as blood drained from my head. Another breath and I was trembling. I knew exactly what was wrong, and I was scared shitless: A newly inverted nipple always meant breast cancer!

I kept staring, sweating, shaking, and wondering what in the hell had happened. I was healthy. I watched what I ate and exercised regularly; how could I have cancer? Damn, it couldn't happen to me! I was a doctor at the top of my field! I know how unreasonable this thought was, but at the time, standing in that steamy bathroom, facing myself in the mirror, it seemed rational. My next thought was: *This only happens to patients, not me.*

And then my knees went weak.

I gripped the counter, took another deep breath and convinced myself I had to calm down. Maybe the nipple inversion was just a temporary condition. I rubbed my chest hard with another towel and looked in the mirror again.

The nipple was still inverted.

More fear rose into my throat. As a doctor I'd been trained to shove my feelings to the side—a necessary trait when doing surgery. I told myself that the most obvious explanation was that the nipple had been inverted for years; I just hadn't noticed it.

But deep down I knew there was no way I wouldn't have noticed something like that. It was *possible*, however, and that made me feel better until I looked in the mirror again.

I had examined more breasts and nipples than I could count: big ones, little ones, saggy, perky, real, and fake. I'd discovered a lot of breast lumps and quite a few cancers. I knew exactly how to do a breast exam on a woman, but I had no idea how to examine a man's breast. Crazy—I'd never even thought about men having breasts.

My thoughts continued to race as I stood there: *What should I look for? What would cancer feel like? If it were cancer, what would I do?* I poked around my nipple, but I was shaking so badly, I could barely touch my chest, much less concentrate or feel anything.

Again I told myself to calm down, but of course I couldn't. I secured the towel around my waist and sneaked down the stairs to the living room bar, poured myself a stiff Jack Daniels, gulped it down, then immediately went back to the bathroom.

The short trip and Jack Daniels combined to settle my nerves just enough to stop my trembling. I stood in front of the mirror again and felt around the nipple. My fingertips immediately found a small mass, the size of a pea, under the inverted nipple. It didn't hurt, but that tiny orb took my breath away, and I began to tremble again.

Chaotic thoughts continued to take over my ability to think like a doctor, and I did something extremely stupid: I tried to pull the inverted portion of the nipple away from the lump. I thought maybe the nipple would just pop out and that would be the end of it.

Of course my inverted nipple didn't pop back out, and I knew that wasn't a good sign. Trembling and sweating more, I checked my breast again in the hope that the lump had magically disappeared, but this tactic didn't work either.

Time seemed to race. I looked at my watch and knew I had to compose myself. I got dressed, met the family downstairs, and kept smiling. But I was hiding the fact that I might be facing my last few months on earth; just beneath the surface, I was crazy with worry. As I stood in our living room, every imagined pain or twinge made me feel like the cancer was growing in my liver, my bones, and my entire body. I was certain I could feel it spreading.

Where could I get it biopsied? Who would do the surgery? What would it feel like to have cancer? And how in the hell would I tell Jenny and the kids I was going to die?

Finally we left for the dinner dance. We found our friends, and I desperately tried to corral my thoughts, but the task was impossible. I turned to gin to constrain the runaway notions filling my head. Every fifteen minutes or so, I went to the men's room, hid in the stall with the door shut, unbuttoned the top of my shirt and felt the lump. It was still there.

Each time I came out of the men's room, I went back to the table, ordered another drink, and danced with Jenny more than I had in ten years. All of this helped distract me, but none of it worked for longer than a few minutes.

I held my wife close and told her again and again that I loved her. I was trying to make up for twenty-eight career-chasing, family-ignoring years all in one night, even though that's impossible.

Then the booze kicked in, and I looked around the hazy, shimmering ballroom. Why the hell did I have breast cancer and all these other people seemed fine? In one afternoon, life had gone from perfect to absolutely unfair. My mind spun completely out of control when Jenny bought one of the auction items for my birthday: a trip around Texas Motor Speedway in a pace car driven by Johnny Rutherford. I actually imagined, maybe even hoped, that when I did take the trip around the race track, we'd slam into a wall going two hundred miles an hour, and I wouldn't have to worry about the damned lump in my breast anymore.

Thankfully, the rest of the night was a blur.

I greeted the next morning with a "gin flu" headache and immense curiosity. The whole lump episode seemed surreal and fuzzy, like a bad dream. Hopeful, I crawled out of bed and headed straight for the mirror. Through hazy, bloodshot eyes, I saw my inverted nipple and felt the lump. My headache didn't matter any longer.

Under stress, my defense mechanisms work extremely well. Like airline pilots, surgeons must remain calm and calculating in the face of adversity. If we can't do that, then we can't do a good job in the operating room. Through seven thousand surgeries, I'd developed a remarkable ability to compartmentalize and stay cool, regardless of what was happening. But now, when my own health was on the line, my cool demeanor grew white-hot, and I melted into a confused, scared patient who was staring at death in the mirror and deciding he'd ignore the problem.

The Sunday forecast was for another beautiful, sunny day. So I took a couple of aspirin, got dressed, and went back to the golf course as if nothing were wrong. I wore my burnt-orange University of Texas golf shirt, which covered my inverted nipple and the lump, and headed out with the old adage, "Out of sight, out of mind."

If I had learned that one of my patients had done this, my face would have grown beet red, the veins in my neck flaring out and almost bursting as I asked the woman why the hell she thought she could ignore something so serious. Now I know why. The implications of what I had discovered the previous night included cancer, surgery, chemotherapy, radiation, metastatic disease, pain, wasting away, and death, and coping with these was simply too overwhelming for anyone, even a doctor.

But unfortunately, the longer we ignore a health issue, the easier it becomes to ignore. I saw that damned inverted nipple every morning and kept telling myself everything would be okay. Oddly, though, the more I saw it, the more convinced I became that it wasn't changing. I soon developed an immense ability to compartmentalize, and my season of denial began.

CHAPTER EIGHT

Denial

For the next three months, I lived in denial. I did everything I normally did: worked hard, played golf as well as I could (I actually have no game at all), kissed Jenny and the kids when I got home, and paid attention to our pets (by then we had added Ernie, formerly a stray cat, to the family). Sometimes I looked in the mirror at my inverted nipple and mashed on it to feel if the lump was still there (it always was), and sometimes I ignored it by throwing my shirt on very quickly. But no matter what I did, I knew, deep down, I had a problem.

A few days after I discovered the lump, I began to convince myself that it was actually getting smaller, and with lumps, smaller is always a good sign. Cancerous lumps get bigger, noncancerous ones get smaller. As it grew smaller in my mind, I told myself it was a cyst and that I should leave it alone because it would eventually shrink to the point where it went away.

Crazy, I know, but as the weeks went by, I continued to have trouble explaining to myself why the nipple remained inverted. Yet I still managed to explain it away. For a few weeks I convinced myself that the inverted nipple just needed a little more time to pop back to normal. Soon, I began to focus on the idea that the lump was benign and I was worrying for nothing. These mind games gave me relief for a little while, but the worry and fear always returned. I was a doctor who had no experience being a patient; I was layered with a thick frosting of fear, and I just kept up the denial. I was so used to a life filled to the brim with work and fixing people, it was easy to distract myself and not worry about my own health.

Yet my doctor side, my medical sense of reason, buried as deeply as it was, managed to surface many times. Every time I stepped out of the shower, my eyes went directly to my right nipple.

Work was my ultimate savior, especially on Mondays. On the first day of the workweek, I always performed multiple surgeries, and I absolutely loved that day. For fifteen years, my normal Monday consisted of five to ten surgical cases, the first commencing at 8:00 a.m. and the last finishing about 10:00 p.m. or later. I chose to operate on Mondays because the operating room was always available, and I could schedule as many cases as I thought I could complete. Mondays were good for the patients, too, although they didn't realize it. Most patients preferred to have surgeries on Thursdays or Fridays so they'd have time to recoup before the next week of work. However, if a medical problem surfaces after a late-week procedure, then the patient is left to seek help at the emergency room, the only available option on weekends. If complications arose after a surgery on Monday, I'd be available for the entire week. By the following weekend, they (and I) were pretty much home free.

One particular anesthesiologist had worked with me for years. Bruce and I had done more than seven thousand surgeries together, and we'd been through a lot of tough, demanding situations. Because of those experiences, we had tremendous respect for each other's abilities. Bruce's sister, Marilyn, was a surgical oncologist who specialized in breast cancer treatment at the University of Texas Southwestern Medical Center at Dallas, where I had a teaching appointment. She and I had met on a few occasions, and I came away very impressed with her knowledge, surgical ability, and forceful personality.

I could have talked to Bruce or his sister about my problem, but I didn't, because I just kept telling myself I was too busy and everything was going to be okay anyway.

I find it amazing now that I didn't do that, but surgery demands such intense concentration that the operating room allowed me to completely repress my worries for hours on end, often until the next day and the next shower.

Tuesdays through Thursdays, I saw forty to fifty patients each day, splitting my time between offices in different parts of Fort Worth. On these days, I encouraged (even demanded) that my patients have a mammogram every year. This was part of my carefully worded discussion of preventive medicine. I signed hundreds of mammogram order forms every week. Every lump I found was evaluated as soon as possible, and every abnormality mammography detected was investigated, no exceptions. Again and again I stressed the importance of these tests. And yet I didn't require this same standard for myself. I just kept denying, procrastinating, and hiding from the truth.

Friday was my "free day." I spent it working on presentations, research, and publications. Most of my presentations were on laparoscopic complications. I constantly told myself there was no way I could take a Friday to get checked out. My preparation work was too important. People were counting on me. Additionally, I had focused on the inverted nipple so many times that it was losing its "fear factor."

My workweek was as full as it could possibly be, a blessing for a person who was trying to avoid thinking about a gigantic health problem. My ego kept assuring me that my job was far too important to take any time off, particularly for something as irrelevant as a benign lump that was shrinking and soon to be gone completely.

I also was exercising for an hour and a half a day, four days a week, starting at 5:30 a.m. These workouts confirmed my earlier conclusion: *I'm in great shape. There's no way someone as fit as I am can have breast cancer, no way.*

I added procrastination to denial. I continually told myself that there would be time *next* week to go to a specialist, if the lump didn't go away before then. But of course my weeks just got busier and the lump never disappeared.

I went from staring at my nipple to just a quick glance, if I thought to before I put my shirt on. I also quit feeling for the lump, because finding it again made the problem all too real, and my fears would resurface.

Another factor was at work, one that was deeper, darker, and took me a long time to face. Twenty years before I found the lump in my breast, my dad's health began to crumble. During the last seven years of his life, his emphysema kept him bedridden with an oxygen cannula strapped around his face, constantly directing oxygen into his nostrils. He could take only very shallow, labored breaths and was cyanotic—slightly blue from a lack of oxygen—all the time. Just breathing was a huge effort for him. Jenny, Julie, and I traveled to Graham frequently to visit, thinking each time would be the last. And each time we visited, I could tell he was miserable.

During a visit two weeks before his death, I sat beside him and he struggled to talk to me, gasping after each word. Suddenly he began to cry and told me he was horribly depressed. His words were crushing.

His crying and confession jarred me. My dad had been the rock of the family for as long as I could remember. He was the one who had challenged me to go to med school. He was always strong, grounded, and accepting. Seeing him this way, learning he was depressed, and not being able to help him was almost more than I could bear.

The next weekend his family doctor admitted him, barely alive, to Graham Hospital. Jenny, Julie, and I headed for Graham. I had the responsibility and duty to talk with his doctor. We discussed doing a tracheostomy and putting him on a respirator, but that would accomplish nothing except prolong his wretched existence. I explained to Dr. Nesbitt, whom I had known for many years, that we wanted only to make my father as comfortable as possible.

Disconsolate, I went back into Dad's room and sat next to his bed for a long time, listening to his labored, painful breaths. I thought about our lives together, how much I loved him, and how, even though I was a doctor, I was totally helpless.

Two hours later Daddy opened his eyes, raised his head off the pillow, looked at me, and said, "I gotta take a piss." Just as quickly, he lay back on the pillow. That was the last thing he said to me. He died eighteen hours later.

Several years earlier, I had made the same decision to stop medical care that was both hopeless and useless for my grandmother and then my grandfather. They died in Graham Hospital, too. But the decision I had to make for my father, and his subsequent death, hit me a lot harder.

The nightmares started the night after his funeral. For the next year or so, every night I woke in a cold sweat, shaking uncontrollably. Over and over, I dreamed that Daddy was lying in his casket and that as I walked closer, he sat up and looked at me with a blank, questioning expression. Every time, I had to tell him he was dead before he would lie back down and be still.

After a year, the terrifying dream finally went away.

But the dream returned the night I discovered my inverted nipple. For the next three months, telling my father to lie back down kept me awake, while my profession kept me occupied during the day. I became exhausted fighting it all, and I knew something had to give.

Eventually it did.

CHAPTER NINE

June 6, 1998: Reality

My fondest memories of childhood center around two activities: dove hunting with my dad and grandfather, and spending weekends at Possum Kingdom Lake, known in Graham as PK. When I was a kid, I dreamed about having my own place there someday.

As soon as it became financially feasible, maybe even a little before, Jenny and I bought a small cabin at PK, complete with a dock, boat, and indoor septic system. There'd be no outhouse for the Johns family! PK is ninety minutes from Fort Worth, and our cabin quickly became our weekend getaway. Jenny, Julie, Jessica, and I thought life was best at PK.

Three months, almost to the day, after I discovered my inverted nipple and lump, Jenny, Jessica, Missy (our second dog), and I loaded up the van early Friday morning and headed off for our first lake outing of the summer. Julie, our oldest daughter, had graduated from Vanderbilt University a few weeks earlier and actually had a job, so she was missing from our group that weekend.

Our first day at the lake started out gorgeous: clear and calm. We spent a couple of hours mopping floors, cleaning toilets, and getting the cabin ready for the summer. That afternoon, as the temperature rose to the low 90s, we loaded our water skis, life jackets, sunglasses, and a cooler full of cold beer and fruit juice into the boat and took off.

The out-of-towners hadn't arrived yet, so PK was quiet and unpopulated. The lake expanded in front of us, smooth as a mirror. It just didn't get any better than that. Jetting through the water was outright exhilarating.

I was wearing my favorite ragged T-shirt and swim trunks. For the past three months, constantly wearing a T-shirt had become a way for me to hide my problem from myself, my family, and everyone else. "Out of sight, out of mind" was working beautifully. The only problem on that Friday was that I never wore a T-shirt to water-ski. While driving the boat to the middle of the lake, I decided that when my turn came, I'd rip off my T-shirt and put my life jacket on really fast so no one, especially not I, would get a chance to see my inverted nipple.

What I wasn't counting on, as it turned out, was good timing and my daughter's ability to fashion another defining moment in my life with an innocent remark—one that I will never forget.

Jessica loves waterskiing as much as I do. On that day she was Christmas-morning excited and couldn't wait to get into the water. As I slowed down in a particularly smooth, protected part of the lake, she bolted to the back of the boat and attached the ski rope before I could get out of my seat. After squirming into her life jacket, she grabbed her slalom ski and plunged into the water.

She got up on the first try with no problem. After a few minutes of skiing, she dropped, swam to the boat and climbed aboard, exuberant and very proud of herself for doing so well.

She wriggled out of her life jacket as I began to take my T-shirt off. Suddenly she reached past me to get a drink out of the cooler. Before she could lift the cooler lid, she stopped and stared at my chest for a split second, then pointed at my nipple and said, "Man, that's ugly."

A chill ran through me.

"What are you talking about?" I shot back.

She pointed at my inverted nipple again and repeated, "Man, that's really ugly."

I felt the blood run out of my face, and then I began to feel light-headed and chilled again. Despite the warm day, a cold sweat formed on my forehead. Sixteen-year-old Jessica's naïve response to my problem immediately shattered my three months of denial and procrastination, and both crashed at my feet.

She had noticed something I had been adamantly denying. Embarrassment clawed at my façade. My own kid was more astute than I had been. In that defining moment, all my lame excuses and every rationale I had conjured went over the side of the boat into the calm water. My sheer foolishness slipped into its place.

From the front of the boat Jenny turned and looked at Jessica and me. "What's ugly?" she asked.

I fumbled with the snaps of my life jacket and finally got the damn thing on, but my legs felt weak. Fortunately a wave came by and rocked the boat a little, helping me to conceal my unsteadiness. I was frantic, desperate to try to regain my composure. Fortunately my years of training in the operating room quickly kicked in.

Steadying myself on the back of the captain's seat, I glanced up, looked at the two of them, laughed, gave them some ridiculous explanation and jumped over the side of the boat before I had to answer any more questions.

But before I even hit the water, the same chill I felt three months earlier, when I discovered my problem, attacked and stayed with me.

After skiing, I climbed out of the water, fully realizing how foolish I'd been. Clarity imposed itself on me. A simple biopsy would clear everything up, and then I wouldn't have to worry anymore. I promised myself I would get one the next week.

I also decided I wouldn't say anything to Jenny. Weird, I know, but I didn't know how to share my fears with anyone. I guess I learned this behavior from my father. Dad never talked about his feelings until a few days before he died, so when I became an adult, I had the same inclination. And I didn't want to worry Jenny or the kids until I knew something concrete. Besides, I *knew* it was nothing.

Oddly, I felt like I was dealing with two people—I was a patient, scared out of his mind and in denial, but I was also a well-trained doctor who knew something was wrong and needed to be addressed.

When we got home from the lake late Sunday night, I sat in our darkened living room and thought about the biopsy that I'd promised myself I would get during the week that was just starting. I'd always been so healthy. Suddenly I realized that this was how patients felt when I explained a diagnosis or when they had problems and didn't come to my office right away.

Before that night, I had never really understood how my patients who had cancer or other serious health problems felt. Sure, I cared deeply for them and wanted to help them as much as I could, but I'd never fully understood their fears or imagined myself in their place.

In our quiet living room, I finally had to face that cancer was scary, even to me. I drew in a deep breath and told myself I was getting a biopsy this week, but then, just as quickly, the other side of me kicked in and I thought, "But of course I don't have cancer."

I didn't sleep much that night.

CHAPTER TEN

June 8, 1998

The moment my alarm startled me awake Monday morning, I slipped right back into denial. I told myself I'd be too busy to get the biopsy that day because I'd be in surgery for twelve hours. So I got up, worked out, showered, checked my inverted nipple and the lump (still there), and then I was off to the operating room by eight.

At the hospital I breathed a sigh of relief when I checked my surgery schedule. I had six cases, so I was certain there was no way to finish in time to get my biopsy. I'd do it tomorrow, or the next day, or maybe the next.

Once I start a surgery, I completely shut out the world for hours at a time. That Monday was no exception. By four in the afternoon I was completing my fifth surgery, a really nasty case of endometriosis that had taken several hours, and I was thinking, "One more case to go. Then it will be 8:00 p.m. and I can go home."

I have always enjoyed listening to country music while I operate. The cadence of the music seems to help me concentrate, particularly during long cases. I was humming along to Willie Nelson's "Whiskey River" and sewing up the last skin incision when my concentration was broken by a voice from the scheduling desk: "Dr. Johns, you're through for the day. Your last case canceled."

Wow! I hadn't finished before 8:00 in months. Then it hit me: *Shit.* Now I had no excuse for not getting the damn thing biopsied.

I finished up the surgery and went out to the waiting room to talk with my patient's family. After answering all their questions, I walked into the surgical dressing room and glanced at my watch. It was only 4:45; I had plenty of time. Finally, the next stage of my journey was about to begin.

To get to the Harris Methodist Hospital breast center, I walked down a couple of flights of stairs, across the glass-walled, plant-filled atrium, then through a long hallway between radiology and the ER. Twice I had to use my prox card to get through locked steel doors. Finally I came to a sign that read "Breast Center," staring at me from above a pair of dark wooden doors. By the time I read those words, I was numb.

The breast center was designed and built by Ralph, a radiologist with special interest and expertise in breast disease. Ralph was in his early forties, slender with a dark complexion and jet-black hair swept back in a greasy ducktail. He was a regular at the fitness center and a casual acquaintance of mine.

Before I opened the door, I hoped they'd be too busy to work me in, or maybe they'd be behind schedule, with dozens of women still in the waiting room. Or maybe they were closed and Ralph was gone for the day or was on vacation.

I glanced up at the sign again and walked toward the doors. Suddenly it felt as if I was about to walk through the giant, gaping, tooth-lined mouth of some terrifying carnivorous animal, ready to suck me in, and I'd never see the light of day again.

But I took a deep breath and walked in anyway.

Damn, the waiting room was empty. At the reception desk sat

a pleasant young woman with dark hair and orange lipstick that matched the color of the "Alan Johns, MD" monogrammed on my coat. Her tattoo, the scaly green head of a fire-breathing dragon, peeked out just above the neckline of her blouse and stared at me. Although she was talking on the phone, she motioned me to the desk.

Soon she hung up, looked at me with a smile, and said, "Can I help you, sir?"

I froze. For three months I had cajoled, rationalized, ignored, repressed, suppressed, and covered up my deepest fears. Now I was about to confront all of them in front of a green, fire-breathing-dragon tattoo.

I cleared my throat and calmed myself. "Is Ralph still here?"

"Ralph?" she asked. "Who's that?"

"Dr. W," I said, realizing she didn't know him by his first name.

"I think he's still here; let me go check." She glanced at my white coat for my name.

In thirty seconds she returned. "Go right on back to his office, Dr. Johns. He's there."

Sweat sprung on my forehead, and my armpits were soaked. I walked the hundred feet to his office, my legs heavy as tree trunks, my heart thumping.

After entering his office, I sat down while Ralph finished some paperwork. Then he looked up, smiled, and said, "What can I do for you, Alan?"

"I need you to take a look at something." My heart continued to race.

"Sure, no problem. When does Jenny want to come in?"

"No, it's me."

He dropped his pen and looked up at me. "Really? What's up?"

Without taking a breath, or so it seemed to me, I filled him in on the past few months.

"Wow," was all he said. Then he rose from his chair and grabbed his white coat, put it on, and said, "Let's take a look." Pointing to his left, he directed me to one of the exam rooms that had been cleaned and readied for the next day.

Alone and scared, I took off my shirt and lay down on the exam table. Ralph finally walked in, turned on the light, and glanced down at my right nipple. Immediately his eyes screamed, "Oh shit!"

These "Oh shit" moments happen frequently to doctors. We might be doing a pelvic exam during a routine annual checkup and find a huge mass that's obviously cancer, or we might be surprised to find a cancerous mass during an ultrasound. "Oh shit" moments can also happen with a routine breast exam, when we discover a hard, irregular mass the patient didn't even know about or a small, inconspicuous mole that is obviously melanoma. The list goes on and on, and these moments happen in every specialty. In a split second the physician knows there's a life-changing medical problem, but the patient has no clue.

Usually doctors have the same reaction to such moments as airline pilots who are anticipating a crash: *Oh shit!* Yet we've been programmed to remain calm, professional, and compassionate, and to come up with a plan. The plan always includes figuring out how to evaluate what we just found.

Simultaneously, and most importantly, we quickly decide how to break the news to the patient. All this happens in a few seconds. Invariably, doctors turn their gaze away because we don't want the patient to see the "Oh shit" look in our eyes, even though most patients don't recognize the look.

Yet every *doctor* is intimately familiar with the unmistakable look in a colleague's eyes. That afternoon, Ralph didn't look away quickly enough. As he silently poked around on my nipple and checked my armpit, I grew more and more fearful. He was looking for an enlarged lymph node. Lymph nodes in the armpit are the first place breast cancer spreads. The simple fact that he was checking my lymph nodes told me he knew exactly what I had, and that fact made me want to jump off the table and run, or maybe just cry, but I couldn't do either.

Finally, after what seemed like an hour, he said, "Yep, there's a little mass just beneath the nipple. Let's do a sonogram."

Ultrasound would determine if the pea-sized lump was cystic and filled with fluid (which is good) or solid with tissue and no fluid (which is bad). I didn't tell Ralph I had tried to sonogram the lump myself a month earlier in my office, after everyone left. Unfortunately, I didn't have the right equipment.

His sonogram technician had already left for the day, so Ralph rolled the beer-cooler-sized ultrasound machine into the room and fired it up. It's good that he brought the machine in. I doubt if I could have gotten myself off the table and remained standing, much less walked to another room.

He squirted some ultrasound-conducting gel on my chest. The gel was really cold, something I needed to remember since I use it on considerably more sensitive areas with my patients.

"Yep, it's solid," he said.

"How about doing a mammogram?" I asked, trembling inside.

"No need. Doesn't matter what a mammogram shows; if there's a solid mass, it needs a biopsy." He stopped for a moment, then looked at me again. "You want to go ahead and do a punch biopsy?"

"Yeah," I forced myself to say, although I was more scared than I'd ever been. "Let's get it over with." Once I had finally decided to face the problem, I wanted answers and I wanted them quickly. "Do it."

Ralph yelled to his nurse, who was trying to get out the back door. She was unlucky enough to be the last nurse to leave that day.

He asked if she wouldn't mind setting up a punch biopsy in room two.

"Sure, no problem," she lied.

When describing a punch biopsy to my patients, I'd always told them that the area would be numbed with Xylocaine first so the biopsy would be "just a little a bee sting, not bad at all." And I'd added that injecting the Xylocaine wouldn't hurt very much either. Ralph regurgitated those exact words as he injected my nipple with Xylocaine. The medication hurt like hell as it went in, like a two-pound, mad-assed hornet with a three foot wingspan, a six-inch stinger, and an attitude. Obviously I needed to alter my explanation a little.

The area seemed pretty numb when Ralph made a little incision in the skin just over the lump. Then he held up the punch biopsy device. It looks exactly like a stainless-steel caulking gun, two feet long, five inches around. The "working end" was the diameter of a small straw and about five inches long. It was pointed, with a hole at the tip for sucking up tissue.

Getting ready to slide the instrument through my incision, Ralph cocked the device the same way one pulls back the hammer on a revolver. It didn't hurt a bit as he slid the instrument through the incision, toward the lump.

Then he uttered those fateful words, "You might feel a little pinch." With that, he pulled the trigger. In that instant, I learned what it feels like to have your breast lifted up with a pair of ice tongs while being simultaneously impaled with a white-hot railroad spike.

A little pinch, my ass!

He pulled the contraption out of my chest as my eyes began to water from the pain. No wonder patients never believe doctors.

I sat up to get a glimpse of the biopsy specimen. The doctor inside me wanted to see what a death sentence looked like. Ralph tried squirting the specimen out of the "stinger" and into a small container filled with formalin, but there wasn't enough tissue for a diagnosis.

He turned to me. "We need to get another sample."

No shit, I thought. "No problem," I lied. "Go ahead."

Ralph cocked the railroad spike again. The second time it felt like smoke should be rising off the damn instrument. But at least I knew what to expect. I braced myself. He cocked the device, hit me again, and it hurt like hell. I couldn't keep the tears from forming in the corners of my eyes.

Now I was pissed. Forget the pain and fear. I was angry at the lump and Ralph. I was mad at the picture hanging on the wall and the electrical plug near the floor. I was even angry at the wall and probably the carpet, too. Mostly, though, I was pissed at myself. The lunacy of the last three months came crashing down on me as all my carefully prepared defense mechanisms collapsed.

Ralph placed a small dressing on my wound. I sat up, put my shirt back on, and sneaked a peek at the small, translucent plastic jar that contained the tiny piece of tissue with such life-altering potential. At that moment life just didn't seem fair.

"You okay?" Ralph asked.

"Sure, I'm fine," I lied again.

"I'll get this sent out this evening. We should have a report back in a couple of days."

My mad was still on. "No thanks," I said as I took the container out of his hand. "I'll just walk it over to Pathology at the hospital."

"But Alan, it's after five."

"No shit," I think I said, but I'm not sure. I was already halfway out the door, specimen in hand, on the way to Pathology.

CHAPTER ELEVEN

Breast Cancer

Most pathology departments are purposefully placed in hospitals. Baylor, Mayo, MD Anderson, Sloan-Kettering, Cleveland Clinic, and Graham General have the same setup: Their pathology departments are buried in the bowels of the building. There's always a windowless, single wooden door at the end of a cold hallway, staving off a particularly unpleasant and slightly acidic odor, and "Pathology" is usually written in fading letters on or just above the locked door.

Pathology departments are located in the recesses of the hospital because visitors and patients don't like to be around sheet-covered bodies being transported to waiting funeral coaches. Neither are people thrilled when confronted by an orderly carrying a glass jug containing some unidentifiable, bloody item freshly removed from a surgery patient.

In larger hospitals, the pathology departments have small satellite labs adjacent to the operating rooms. These labs are processing centers for tissue samples that require an immediate diagnosis, while the patient is still asleep on the operating table. In these labs a "frozen section diagnosis" is made by rapidly freezing a biopsy specimen, then cutting off a paper-thin slice and examining it immediately under the microscope. A presumptive diagnosis can then be relayed to the surgeon right away.

After I left the breast center, I headed to the satellite lab because the Harris Methodist pathology department always closed precisely at 5:00 p.m. The satellite lab, however, was staffed until the surgery schedule had been completed, regardless of the time of day, because surgeons never know when they might need a frozen section diagnosis.

I had no intention of waiting for an answer until tomorrow or any other day. The surgery schedule was full, which would keep Fred, the pathologist assigned to the satellite pathology lab, working for several more hours.

The walk back to the hospital seemed quick and easy because I felt relieved. Finally I had done *something*. As I walked across the parking lot and into the main building, I reserved a faint hope that by removing that little piece of tissue, I had fixed my health problem. Deep down I knew that was unlikely, but the thought helped me make the trek over to the pathology lab.

The satellite pathology lab at Harris was a rectangular room, twenty feet by thirty feet, painted light blue and lined with stainless-steel equipment. To the right sat a small doctor's office with a desk piled high with texts and journals. Adjacent to the doctor's office was a narrow room with a bench attached to one wall. Two large microscopes, each with two viewing heads (allowing two pathologists to look at the same slide simultaneously), rested on the bench.

As I walked into the lab, it looked like a science fiction movie set, eerie and foreboding. I swallowed hard and glanced around some more. I'd been in the same place that morning with a patient's biopsy and noticed nothing, but now all I saw were syringes, scalpels, and cutting boards covering every available countertop. The people working in the lab looked like aliens with scrub suits on underneath bulky, disposable blue surgical gowns. They wore double gloves and shoe covers that came to their knees. Surgical caps covered their heads, and face masks sporting large, plastic splash shields protected their faces—they looked like a hazmat team dressed in blue.

The pathology technician greeted me. "Hey, Dr. Johns, you have another specimen for us?" His breath condensed inside the plastic shield, making him and the area even more surreal.

"Maybe. Is Fred around?"

"He's in his office."

Fred was a single, fifty-year-old, extremely knowledgeable pathologist who still lived with his mother. He was quiet, shy, balding, and plump, with a round cherubic face on which rested a pair of thick-rimmed glasses that had been fashionable in the 1950s. He loved opera, ballet, the symphony, and small fragments of humans, living or dead. He was a typical pathologist—he was dedicated and worked well with surgeons, but he didn't care much for direct interaction with patients. He also loved blood, guts, body parts, microscopes, and pungent odors.

I respected Fred for what he did. He was a vital and necessary part of the medical process. Most treatment recommendations and decisions rely heavily on the pathologist's work and diagnoses.

I found Fred sitting at his desk, engrossed in one of his pathology journals. The tech to whom I'd spoken when I walked in had followed me to his office. "Hey, Fred," I said. "I need you to look at something for me."

He glanced up at the surgery schedule. "Sure. Which patient?"

For the second time in the past thirty minutes, I confessed, "It's me."

Fred put down his journal. He was clearly uncomfortable, but I was blocking the door and not about to leave without a diagnosis, even if it was only a preliminary one.

"Well, okay, what's going on?" Fred asked.

I handed him the specimen container and explained the situation to him and the tech. As my story progressed, Fred's face began to lose color. He stood and brushed past me, then gave the container to his tech and said, "Get a couple of frozen sections of this."

I expected Fred to turn back, but he walked out the door, turned right, and began walking aimlessly down the hall. I grabbed a chair by one of the microscopes, sat, and tried to stay calm. The lab had always been cold, but it felt like I was sitting in my dad's grocery freezer—cold, dark, and ominous.

The technician kept his head down, eyes steady on his work, desperately trying to ignore me. I sat waiting as the seconds ticked by. For someone who had procrastinated for three months, five minutes seemed like an eternity.

Finally the tech had three slides ready. Still unable to look at me, he slid the first one under the microscope, laid the other two on the table, walked over to the intercom, and paged Fred, who was pacing impatiently up and down the hall to avoid talking with me.

I sneaked a look at the first slide as cold sweat began to accumulate on my forehead. Damn, it had been twenty-five years since I took pathology in Galveston, and I didn't remember much. I had studied a lot of slides during residency, but that was a long time ago, and we never looked at breast tissue. I might as well have been looking at a fried egg. At least I could have identified that. I stared at the slide and convinced myself the cells looked completely normal. The lump was probably a benign fibroadenoma.

Fred walked in, sat down at the left microscope lens, and began looking through the eyepiece. He was on my good-eye side, so I could watch him out of the corner of my eye while pretending to study the slide.

He didn't say a word; he just breathed heavily, let out an occasional groan, and then went back to concentrating.

All I could think was, *Come on, asshole, say "benign fibroadenoma"!* How difficult could that be?

The longer he studied the slide, the more frantic, sweaty, and agitated I became. Then his breathing slowly became more rapid. A distinct drop of sweat formed on his balding forehead, and his eyes shifted.

Damn!

I started shivering.

He stood up; glanced at me, pupils dilated; then said, "I'll be back in a minute." It was the second time in thirty minutes that I had seen the unmistakable *Oh shit* look.

His few words sent more chills through my body.

Fred was a fantastic pathologist, and many times he'd signed his name on a pathology report with the word cancer written all over it. But I guess he'd never spoken that word directly to a patient. Obviously he couldn't do it now.

A couple of minutes later, Fred walked back into the lab with Julie, another pathologist. He must have called her up from the main lab, where she had finished her day and was desperately trying to leave. Julie was in her late forties with bright red hair (natural, of course) and a very pleasant personality. Since she was responsible for most of our GYN pathology work, I knew her well.

Fred had summoned her to look at the slides with him, and, I figured, to tell me the bad news.

"How you doing, Alan?" she asked, sitting down at the microscope.

"Fine," I lied, trying to keep my teeth from chattering. The room was growing colder, and I felt as if I was going to jump out of my skin.

Staring down into the eyepieces, she said, "Man, I don't like the looks of this."

I made a quick mental note: Never use those words with a patient in the room.

"It looks like a ductal cell carcinoma, probably grade two," were her next words.

That's when the blood rushed out of my head, and I could barely sit up. Cancer, grade two!

Julie looked up from the microscope as Fred was making a hasty exit again.

There it was, exactly what I had known (but denied) for months: ductal cell carcinoma.

My pulse raced and my blood pressure soared. What had been a very cold room a minute earlier suddenly became uncomfortably hot, stuffy, and claustrophobic.

A thousand thoughts raced through my mind all at once, but only one kept resonating, like an echo that just wouldn't quit: *I have cancer.*

Julie stood and laid a hand on my shoulder. "Alan, I'm sorry, but you know frozen sections can sometimes be wrong. I'll process the entire specimen and we'll call you tomorrow morning. Maybe I'm wrong."

I was sweating, trembling, and hyperventilating. I desperately wanted to regain some measure of composure, yet I could hardly breathe. I *had* to get out of that room, out of the building, out of the whole damn building!

I may have said "thanks" as I bolted, but I doubt it. The next thing I remember is sitting behind the wheel of my car in the physician's parking lot, crying. I guess that had to happen before I could move on.

Finally I felt sufficiently in control to head home. I drove on autopilot, my mind spinning in a thousand different directions. I was consumed by dozens of patient questions and doctor decisions that had to be made. Fear was temporarily replaced by frenzy.

How was I going to tell Jenny and the girls? What was going to happen to me? What would cancer be like? Would I be able to work? Had I performed my last surgery? Could we make it financially? Then really sobering thoughts assaulted me: How long would I live? And: What would it be like to die?

It took fifteen minutes to get home, but I don't remember the drive. I do remember pulling into the garage and wondering where Jenny and the kids were.

The sixteen steps from the garage to our house were usually easy to climb, but at that moment it seemed like two miles. Jenny, Jessica, and Julie (who had joined us for dinner) were home, but I was in such a haze that I don't remember where they were or what they were doing.

I found Jenny in the kitchen. She looked up and instantly knew something was wrong. I stared at her, scared and trembling, and said, "We need to talk."

In twenty-eight years of marriage, I had never uttered those words, and they must have scared the devil out of her.

"I've got breast cancer," I blurted.

There, I said it! Finally I was admitting what I'd known for months.

Jenny looked stunned and terrified. Tears formed in her eyes, and we cried together. Then, suddenly, the tears stopped, she took a deep breath, put her hands on my shoulders, looked me directly in the eye, and said, "Doesn't matter. We'll get through it."

Her attitude and strength of character have always defined her. Fiercely protective, she simply refused to let anything threaten her family. In that instant she decided that breast cancer would be no different. Her attitude and support gave me a lot of strength to face what lay ahead.

We held each other for a while, saying nothing, then called the kids to come downstairs.

Jessica and Julie sauntered into the kitchen, mildly annoyed that we had interrupted whatever it was they were doing. But one quick look at us was all they needed to know that something was up and it wasn't good.

We went outside and sat down on the back porch. Our family always found the outdoors comforting, and it seemed the appropriate place to tell our children that we were in for some rough times.

I tried to be as reassuring as possible, but all they heard was "cancer." Julie, twenty-one, and Jessica, sixteen, were both old enough to understand the implications and young enough to be completely horrified. Sitting on that hard concrete porch, tears flowing uncontrollably, I told them everything I knew.

Unfortunately it wasn't much, but I repeated what they needed to hear: I was not going to die.

They believed it, but Jenny and I knew that with a diagnosis this serious, nothing was certain.

Later that night I went to bed with one small sliver of hope, unrealistic though it was. Fred and Julie were going to look at the permanent slides the next morning. Maybe their initial diagnosis of the frozen section was wrong.

As I lay in bed, the only thing I knew for certain was that I'd waited too long. I didn't sleep much that night, and when I did, the nightmare about my father returned.

CHAPTER TWELVE

June 9, 1998

I gave up trying to sleep about five thirty and quietly got out of bed. Jenny had been up with me most of the night because every thirty minutes or so I would startle awake, soaked in a cold sweat. The nightmare about my father kept recurring, and sometime in the middle of the night, I became the one in the coffin instead of Daddy. Each time I awoke, Jenny held me and repeated, "We'll get through this." She had managed to fall asleep about five, and I didn't want to wake her, so I quickly put on my running gear.

I walked outside expecting to find a world that had stopped since my life had been turned upside down, but as I jogged down the driveway in the familiar morning darkness, the crisp morning breeze touched my face right on schedule. To my surprise the neighborhood was no different than yesterday. And the sun began to show through the lush trees as if nothing had happened to me. I still felt shocked and upset, but the normalcy of the world outside my door was my first clue that things might just work out all right.

I did my usual run and showered, and then Jenny awoke and we talked. We decided I would call her as soon as I got the final diagnosis from Fred. If I had cancer I was going to choose a surgeon I respected, one who had done a lot of mastectomies. I needed a plan, and it had to begin that morning.

But my experience with breast cancer was limited to breast examinations, mammograms, and referring patients to a specialist or a surgeon if they needed a mastectomy. This sounds like a simple protocol, but it isn't. By 1998, I had done more than seven thousand surgeries, operated with dozens of local gynecologists and general surgeons, reviewed hordes of videotaped surgeries, and had been an expert witness for hundreds of medical malpractice cases. Through all of that, it had become abundantly clear to me that there were not many surgeons to whom I would send my patients, my family, or myself. So when I referred my newly diagnosed breast cancer patients to a surgeon, the referral was a carefully considered recommendation based on direct knowledge of that surgeon's ability, not just a phone number and an office address.

Referring patients for surgery is extremely important, and I took referrals very seriously. My own referral would be no different.

By the time I finished hospital rounds and was pulling into my parking space at the office, I had my course of action narrowed down to a simple, linear path that I felt comfortable with. Even though I was an experienced doctor, I was still thinking like a patient. As a physician, I knew that the most important aspects of my decisions would be, first, not to rush into surgery, and second, to have a health care advocate—someone to help me think my way through this. As a patient, I wanted the damn thing out tomorrow (at the latest)!

If my diagnosis was breast cancer (I was still holding out hope), I had decided to simply call a surgeon in Fort Worth whom I trusted and schedule my mastectomy. I was in such shock that I hadn't even considered going to Dallas for an evaluation by a surgical oncologist. Like most of my patients in the same situation, all I could think about was that I wanted to get the damn thing cut out as soon as possible.

I climbed out of my car and went into the office ready to see patients. During the past few years, I had become very skilled at ignoring the rest of the world while I was in the exam room with a patient, and I figured I would be able to function like that on this day, too. But once the day started, I found that each time the phone rang, my heart raced and I lost concentration in anticipation of the call from Fred. All I wanted to hear were the few simple words, "Sorry, Alan, we were mistaken; it's just a little benign fibroadenoma."

Finally the "Sorry, Alan" call came, but the words that followed stopped me cold.

"It's an invasive ductal cell carcinoma, grade two," Fred said. "Julie looked at the slides and agrees. Invasive ductal cell carcinoma," he repeated. But he didn't have to. I understood every word, much more than I wanted to.

As if the words "breast cancer" weren't enough, he'd added "invasive" and "grade two." Those adjectives may not mean much at first to most patients, but they spoke volumes to me. Invasive meant the cancer was not confined to one little rubber-ball lump. No, it was invading surrounding tissue, nerves, and blood vessels.

As for grade two, tumors are graded on a scale from one to three based on how abnormal they look and how likely they are to spread. Grade one tumors are the least aggressive and most likely to be cured. Mine was not grade one.

My nurses heard the phone slam down. Theresa looked into my office and asked, "Boss, are you okay?"

"Yeah," I lied, as I got up and shut the door. I sat back down, both elbows on my desk, my head in my hands. *Well, that's it, no more hiding from it.*

I called Jenny to let her know there was no escape. The diagnosis was Final with a capital "F."

With unmistakable determination in her voice, she said, "Okay, let's get it fixed. When are you coming home?"

"In a little while," I answered. "I really don't feel like seeing patients, and we've got a lot to do."

"I love you," she said before hanging up.

My mind kept spinning. There were so many things to decide. Unlike my patients, I knew (or thought I knew) what had to be done. I needed to make the final decision about who was going to perform the surgery and when. Plus I had a business to run and people who depended on me for care. My office and surgery schedules would have to be revised, and the sooner that was completed, the better for both my patients and me. Finally, my fear had been replaced by rational, organized thinking. To get this all started, I had to let my nurses know what was going on.

Office nurses are one of the most integral cogs in a doctor's practice, and my five nurses were no different. Some had worked with me for fifteen years. We were as much friends as co-workers.

When I opened my office door, I found them gathered in the hallway, wondering what the hell was going on. Theresa, one of the nurses who had been with me for years, was the leader. An attractive, bright-eyed, ebullient, and caring lady, she was in charge of my infertility practice. Because of her, everyone called me "Boss."

"What's up, Boss?" she asked. "You don't look so good."

"You guys come in here. We need to talk."

After they sat down, I explained that I had breast cancer and would need surgery, but didn't know when it would take place or how long I would be out of the office. We needed to cancel patients for the afternoon so I could set things up.

I studied their astonished expressions for a moment, and then we all began tearing up.

"Breast cancer?" Theresa asked, disbelief weighing down her words.

"Yeah, breast cancer."

After the shock passed, we discussed our priorities. First, we had to take care of our patients who had immediate and ongoing problems. Next, we needed to reschedule those coming in for routine checkups. Last, we needed a plan for night and after-hours coverage when I couldn't be available.

"What should we tell our patients?" Theresa asked, wondering if I wanted anyone to know what was happening.

"Tell them the truth." I was completely fed up with lying to myself or anyone else.

"When should we start canceling your schedule?" she continued, her voice a little shaky.

"I'll try to get a date for my surgery this afternoon, so let's wait until tomorrow. But it'll be soon." I stood and headed out the door.

With that simple statement, I mirrored the attitude of most patients who have just been given a cancer diagnosis. All have the same thought: *I want to see somebody now—any doctor who will operate tomorrow will be just fine. Just get the damn thing out of me.*

Only later did I learn how dangerous such a hasty decision can be.

"Who are you going to see?" Jenny asked when I arrived home.

My choice of a surgeon had been my primary concern all morning. I'd decided to call a friend who I respected and knew to be an excellent surgeon. I wanted to find out if he could get me on his schedule for a mastectomy next week. My the-sooner-the-better attitude was in full swing. I had started dialing his office number when Jenny spoke up.

"I think you should talk to Bruce's sister," she said before I pressed the last number.

I hung up, embarrassed that I was in such shock and panic that I hadn't thought of my anesthesiologist friend and his sister, Marilyn, who was a surgical oncologist specializing in breast cancer at University of Texas Southwestern Medical Center at Dallas. It would be reassuring if she agreed with my plan to have the mastectomy done by my friend the next week. I wasn't particularly interested in going to Dallas for surgery, but her opinion would be welcome. Thanks to Jenny's suggestion, I stopped and decided—fatefully, it turned out—to give her a call.

I called Bruce, let him know what was going on, and got Marilyn's number. He was really empathetic and concerned and was certain his sister would be happy to talk with me. I left a message with her secretary at two-thirty. Marilyn was in surgery and would get back to me when she finished.

I waited eight hours, fully expecting that Marilyn would tell me to go ahead with my plan. I was in for another little surprise when she returned my call.

"Hey, Marilyn, thanks for calling," I said, shaking like an intern trying to hit a vein with a needle for the first time. Jenny was listening on another phone.

"Bruce called, said you have a problem," Marilyn said.

I explained my entire saga.

"You waited three damn months!" she said, almost screaming. She sounded like a stern mother reprimanding her child. Marilyn was not known for her tact.

"Yeah, I guess I did," I replied in a quiet, squeaky voice. "Pretty stupid, huh?"

"Yes, well, anyway, you need to have your sentinel nodes done, too."

Revealing my newfound ignorance, I asked, "What the hell is a sentinel node?"

She explained that breast cancer spreads to a patient's lymph nodes first, then through the rest of the body. If the "sentinel node" (the first node that drains a tumor) can be identified, then it can be removed and analyzed while a patient is still on the operating table. If the sentinel node is cancer-free, the tumor probably hasn't spread anywhere else, negating a need for further surgery.

"If we find cancer in the sentinel node, you'll need a full axillary lymph node dissection along with your mastectomy," she said. "But identifying the sentinel node can be tricky, and you shouldn't let just any surgeon do it."

I had successfully repressed any possibility that the cancer had spread beyond my nipple. Sure, I had thought about it, feared it, but I hadn't really come face-to-face with the idea. I'd been ready to schedule a mastectomy, forgetting or ignoring that I might need removal of my axillary lymph nodes (known as "lymph node dissection").

I'd repressed any thoughts about the lymph node excision for other reasons, too. An axillary lymph node dissection would carry a considerable risk of lifelong lymphedema in my right arm, my operating arm. With a permanently swollen right arm and hand, my surgical career would be over, and I wouldn't be able to support my family. And if the nodes were full of cancer, my life would be over, period.

The seriousness of my situation was becoming more obvious by the second, and a hasty decision could be life-altering and quite possibly fatal. Realizing I needed a lot of information from a reliable, trained, and experienced source, I made a quick but life-changing decision of a different type, thanks to my wife's suggestion.

"Would you mind if I come over to see you and figure this out?" I asked Marilyn.

"Sure, come on over. I'll be happy to talk with you and Jenny."

I hung up the phone. Jenny and I looked at each other. Almost simultaneously we said, "Here we go."

I called Marilyn's office first thing the next morning and made an appointment to see her two days later, on Thursday at 9:00 a.m.

With that simple conversation, my future, and ultimately the future of breast care in Fort Worth, Texas, was forever altered.

CHAPTER THIRTEEN

UTSMC–Dallas

The Tuesday and Wednesday before I went to see Marilyn were filled with my patients' problems, keeping me fully occupied. Although I was finally out of denial, I still worried about what lay ahead and was anxious to hear what Marilyn had to say. I had met Marilyn a few years earlier and found her to be a truly unique individual. She was in her early forties, about five foot five, slender with short, brown, curly hair, and she wore no makeup. Her demeanor was professional and to the point. The first time we met, her dark brown eyes focused on me and commanded my attention. Later I noticed that she did this with everyone. She was quite possibly the most serious, intense, intimidating individual I have ever met.

My second encounter with Marilyn had taken place about a year later. I was in the men's dressing room adjacent to the operating suites at Parkland Hospital, getting ready to change into scrubs so I could help some residents with a laparoscopy. At the time, I was working with the OB-GYN residents at Parkland only twice a month, so no one knew who I was. I'm sure most of the people at the hospital thought I was an instrument salesman.

As I was pulling on my scrubs, three young men walked up to adjoining lockers. They were engrossed in a conversation, oblivious to anyone else around. Overhearing their discussion, I learned they were general surgery residents assigned to Marilyn's service, and they were headed over to the surgery clinic to see patients under her supervision. From my conversations with Bruce, her brother, I was well aware of Marilyn's reputation among the residents: They described her as talented, demanding, unapologetic, and relentless. She leapt on their mistakes with exuberance and pointed out every error in minute detail. Anyone starting her rotation with any hint of arrogance had absolutely none by the time she was finished with them.

The three male residents continued to rant about the "raving bitch" they would have to endure that afternoon. She was a real pain in the ass and the only female surgeon in the division, which just made her demeanor worse in their little minds.

My smile grew as I took in every word, and I salivated at the possibilities. As soon as they were gone, I picked up the phone and asked the hospital operator to page Marilyn. She answered quickly.

"Hey, Marilyn. It's Alan Johns, Bruce's friend," I said. "We met about a year ago."

"Hi, what can I do for you?"

"Listen, you've got three residents on the way over, pretty green ones, I'd bet."

"Yeah, they just started two weeks ago," she said, then added, "They're really full of themselves."

"Want to have some fun?"

"Sure."

"These guys need to learn that at Parkland, the walls have ears."

I repeated the conversation I had just overheard, particularly the "raving bitch" part. By the time I'd finished, she was laughing so hard she could barely talk.

"This is going to be fun," she said, her laughter conveying delight.

I never heard what she did to those three, and I'm sorry I couldn't be a fly on the wall when they sauntered into the clinic. I would bet, however, that their "Hello, Dr. L" was met with a response they weren't expecting. I would also wager that they had an interesting afternoon while learning a very valuable lesson.

The next time I found myself in Dallas talking with Marilyn, it wasn't nearly as much fun.

Marilyn's office was a forty-five minute drive from our house. Jenny and I were up early on that clear, beautiful Thursday, eager to get on with this, and ready (or so we thought) for what lay ahead.

UT Southwestern Medical Center is a sprawling, irrationally designed mess of a campus consisting of newer structures interspersed with faded, antiquated buildings. None had any identifying marks, and there was no discernable logic to the layout—it's a maze no rational person would design, much less try to navigate. Fortunately I had a few years' experience there, so Jenny and I found our way to the breast center without too much trouble.

As I walked into the waiting room of the breast center, the completion of my transformation from doctor to patient began, although I didn't realize it at the time. That transition ultimately proved to be fascinating, scary, and even fun, but it forever changed my perspective about medicine and life.

I was more scared than anything, but relieved finally to be getting something done. So my sense of humor, which is usually keen anyway, was in high gear.

I signed in at the reception desk under a long list of patients already waiting—although I didn't count, I figured I was somewhere around number ninety-nine! Jill (the receptionist) handed me what seemed to be a hundred pages of paperwork to complete and sign. Staring at the one-inch stack, I wondered if I would live long enough to complete the task. I sat in the chair next to Jenny and began reading and answering questions. When I was finished, I walked back up and put the papers on Jill's desk.

"We'll call you in a minute. Just take a seat," Jill said.

Yeah, I'll bet it'll be a minute, I thought, remembering how many times my receptionist must have said the same thing, knowing that the wait would be a few hours, not minutes.

When I sat beside Jenny again, she smiled and asked, "Having fun yet?"

I scowled, my right hand still contorted from writer's cramp. All I could think about was how useless the paperwork was. The same stupid questions were asked a dozen different ways, and I wondered if *anyone* ever read the forms before signing them.

After what seemed like a six-hour wait, I thought I heard a "Mr. Johns" from the reception desk. Actually it sounded more like "Mister" followed by a bunch of unintelligible gibberish, as if spoken by the person taking my order at a drive-through burger place. Since I was the only "Mister" in the breast center, I stood and ambled up to the receptionist.

Smiling at me like we'd been friends for years, Jill said, "Good morning, Mr. Johns. We're sending you downstairs for a mammogram, then Dr. L will see you afterwards."

My nerves calmed a bit as my sense of humor kicked into overdrive. I couldn't help but grin. A guy in an otherwise female-only mammogram unit was going to be an event. "Where do I go?" I asked.

"Down the stairs to the second floor. Lori will take you." Jill gestured to a pleasant young lady standing next to her. Lori smiled and directed me toward the door labeled "Fire Exit Only."

"Is there a fire and we're the only two getting out?" I asked, trying to lighten the situation a little.

"No," she said. Obviously she wasn't amused. "We can't take the elevator," she whispered as if we were planning to rob a bank. "The fire exit opens into a stairwell that leads to a back door of the mammography center downstairs. We're going in the back way so the other patients won't see you. Our unit manager thinks a man in the mammogram area might freak out some of the patients."

I nodded and followed her down the stairs, imagining an announcement coming over the intercom: "May I have your attention, please. Man on the floor! Man on the floor! Ladies, hide your tits!"

I laughed, and Lori glanced back at me sheepishly. She had no idea I was a gynecologist who had seen approximately fifty pairs of breasts every day for the past eighteen years, so another pair wouldn't be that interesting. However, my imagination was lit, and I began to wonder if Dallas breasts might look different than Fort Worth breasts. But because we were going in the back door to the mammogram center, there was little chance my one good eye would be exposed to any.

Two flights down, we exited the stairwell. Lori opened the designated fire exit for the mammogram dressing rooms and motioned me ahead of her. "Thanks," I said as I walked through the doorway. Suddenly I heard a gasp, looked up, and saw a rather large pair of distinctly bare Dallas breasts.

They look pretty much the same as the Fort Worth ones, I thought.

The owner of the breasts looked at me, crossed her arms over her chest, eyes wide and mouth agape as if she'd just come face-to-face with Jack the Ripper. I think she was about to let loose a blood-curdling scream when I said, "It's fine—I'm a gynecologist." I'm sure she found that comforting.

"Shit!" Lori said under her breath before she hustled me into one of the dressing rooms. "Take your shirt off. Betty will be with you in a minute. And don't leave the dressing room," she commanded as she handed me a feminine, flowery gown.

"Does it open back or front?" I asked, laughing as she slammed the door shut. A moment later I heard her hurry out the fire exit. I removed my shirt, put on my cute gown, sat, and waited. After a while I got bored and stood up, but I realized there was no place to go. The powers that be wouldn't let me sit out in the waiting room with the other patients. I looked down at my flowery gown and figured that being sequestered was probably better. And it did keep me from scaring the hell out of any more women.

After what seemed like another six hours, Betty flung open the door and asked, "Mr. Johns?"

"Yes."

"Follow me." Betty was about sixty-five, plump, gray-haired, and angry. Tobacco stains covered every fingernail. She wore a white uniform that was tattered and discolored around the collar. Wrinkles etched her face, and her lips were pulled into a perpetual frown. I'm not sure what she was angry about, but I doubt she needed a reason.

She directed me down a narrow, short hall to the mammogram room. I walked in and stopped. The mammogram machine looked like a medieval, stainless-steel torture device with two large, cold, metal flat plates ready to mash whatever got in their way. A large metal crank lurked on the right side.

"Put your right breast on this plate," she ordered, pointing to the metal plates. She was obviously not one for small talk. I followed her orders. Then she grabbed the crank and began to lower the top plate, squishing the entire right side of my chest between the "jaws of death." Betty didn't seem to care if a few ribs got caught in the middle; she was concerned only that *something* got between those plates, and anything seemed to be fine with her.

Suddenly it felt as if a large brick were sitting on top of my chest. She continued to crank the two plates toward each other, mashing muscle and tissue into what felt like a bloody mess. The only thing to which I can compare this experience is what I imagine it would be like to place my breast on the kitchen table between two concrete bricks and have an NFL lineman jump up and down on them. I was trying to suppress a scream when Betty suddenly decided to strike up a conversation:

"Well now, Mr. Johns, what do you do for a living?"

I took a deep breath to keep from making a fool out of myself. Without really thinking, I answered truthfully (torture can have that effect). "I'm a gynecologist," I replied in a squeaky, strained voice.

She stopped and stared at me for a second, and then a wicked grin appeared. A moment later she began mumbling, "Gynecologist, gynecologist, gynecologist." With each repetition, she cranked the handle down another turn as if she were trying to draw blood. Like a mouse with its tail caught in a trap, I was stuck—I couldn't get away without leaving a chunk of my chest between those plates.

Suddenly Betty came out of her trance, laughed, and said, "You might feel a little pressure, *Doctor Johns*." That's when I realized I should be more careful about revealing my occupation in this place.

"Gynecologist, gynecologist, gynecologist," she kept repeating as I took another deep breath.

After what seemed like an hour, she loosened the vice. The relief was instantaneous as the blood rushed back into my flesh. As I took my first relaxed breath, Betty smiled and said, "Now, Doctor, let's do the left side. You'll only feel a little pressure."

After "Betty the Masher" finished both sides, I finally escaped, battered and bruised, crawled back up the stairs, and found Jenny in the waiting room.

"How did it go?" she asked.

"Mammograms suck!" I replied, checking my shirt for bloodstains for the tenth time.

"Really? I wouldn't know." She laughed.

After another seemingly six-hour wait, the receptionist called me again. I went to the desk and asked sarcastically, "Will this be painful?"

"Hopefully not, Mr. Johns. Go into room three. Dr. L. will be with you in a moment."

In a moment, my ass, I thought. Jenny and I went into the examination room and sat quietly. Finally the door opened and Marilyn walked in. Still in her scrubs and doctor's coat, she'd just come from surgery. We shook hands and she introduced herself to Jenny.

"How you doing?" she asked as she sat down in front of us. She was still just as intense as I remembered.

"Okay," I lied.

She explained that she needed to do a quick exam, so I took off my shirt and checked it yet again for bloodstains. Marilyn kept grumbling something about "three damn months" as she examined my breast. When she finished, I sat up and we began discussing the sentinel node procedure. She explained that sentinel node technology might help me avoid axillary node dissection and the complications associated with it.

To identify the sentinel node, a radioactive substance is injected into the tumor along with some blue dye. Several hours later, a scanner is used to find the lymph node nearest the tumor that contains the radioactive marker. Once the node has been identified, its location is marked by placing an "X" on the overlying skin with an indelible marker—a very important "X marks the spot."

During surgery the skin will be opened through the "X," and the lymph node beneath this mark is removed. If the node is stained with blue dye, that is further confirmation that it is, indeed, the sentinel node—the first lymph node that's draining the tumor.

The node then goes to the pathology lab for a frozen section analysis. If no cancer is found within the node, it is assumed that the cancer has not spread elsewhere. Just as important, the need for chemotherapy and/or radiation therapy depends on what is found in this node. The information is also critical for accurately staging the cancer (determining how much it has spread), which helps estimate the chances of cure.

After listening intently, I asked Marilyn if the lymph node is ever mistakenly identified as sentinel when it is actually not the first to drain the tumor. She nodded.

"What if it's really *not* the sentinel node and the cancer has already spread beyond it through another node?" I asked.

Marilyn explained that then the supposed sentinel node is "falsely negative." In this situation, the cancer has spread, but no one knows. As a result, the patient might be undertreated, and the chances of cure would greatly decrease. She talked about a surgeon's need to know how often (within his or her practice, hospital, and radiology setting) a sentinel node is "falsely negative," and about the guidelines that help answer that question. Marilyn explained that her own false-negative rate was 2 percent, which was excellent.

Accurate identification of this first node requires a cooperative effort between the surgeon and radiologist, so they usually work as a team. In their first twenty to fifty patients, this team identifies the sentinel node, surgically removes it, and then performs a full axillary node dissection. When this group of patients is finished and has been evaluated, the team knows how often they identified a sentinel node as being free of cancer when, in reality, the cancer had already spread beyond the sentinel node. This gives them their false-negative rate. This number varies from team to team, and it is potentially life-saving information. Before surgeons offer sentinel node technology to breast cancer patients, they should know the false-negative rate for their team.

It was obvious that accurate identification of the sentinel node was absolutely critical and required an extraordinary combination of experience and cooperation between the radiologist and surgeon. If I wanted to maximize my chances of cure and at the same time take advantage of this technology and possibly avoid axillary node dissection and lymphedema, the surgery had to be done in Dallas. For a person who had almost scheduled a mastectomy for the next week, the conversation with Marilyn had been sobering.

Marilyn explained what would happen before surgery, what the mastectomy entailed, how the first few days after surgery would go, and how many days I would be hospitalized. We even talked a little about how long I would be off work. Jenny remembered her saying I would be off for five or six weeks, but I'm certain she said two weeks. Interesting how that works.

Then there was silence. Jenny and I looked at each other.

"Any questions?" Marilyn asked.

"When can we get this scheduled?" I asked.

"When do you want to do it?" she countered.

"Today."

"Nice try, Alan. That's not going to happen."

"Tomorrow?" I tried again.

"How about next Wednesday?" she offered.

"I can make that work," I said as I reluctantly gave up on

tomorrow. With that, we thanked Marilyn and left. Her office would call me with all the details.

As we walked back to the car, I stopped, looked at Jenny, and said, "Damn, this is a little scary. Those nodes really need to be clear."

"Yeah, but we don't have a choice, so forget about that. Let's just do it."

Having done so many surgeries in the same operating room with the same anesthesiologist and a great team of nurses, I was extremely comfortable in my own little surgical world. The key words were *my own*. I knew nothing about the system in which Marilyn operated. I was going to be in her arena, not mine, and I found that very disconcerting and frightening.

My fear grew as we drove the 30 miles home. I was going to be admitted to a strange hospital, have surgery in an unfamiliar operating room, and be taken care of by people I didn't know. Until then, it had never occurred to me that my patients lived every day with these fears.

That really sucked.

CHAPTER FOURTEEN

Support and Surgery

By the time Monday morning arrived, news of my problem had leaked out to our friends. Our phone rang constantly, and the outpouring of support, concern, well-wishes, and offers of help was both overwhelming and uplifting. Support systems become extremely important when these things occur, and family members need support as much, maybe even more, than the patient. I knew that women often have tremendous support systems, and since my immediate family was all female, our phone kept ringing.

Monday afternoon, however, my support system showed up. I was sitting at my desk, finishing some paperwork after seeing a patient. The receptionist let me know that Dr. G was on the line and wanted to talk to me. I had first met Art G when he started his OB-GYN residency at John Peter Smith the year after I finished. When I began my private practice, I also did some part-time teaching for the John Peter Smith Hospital residents program. Art and I had worked together for a few months and quickly became friends. He had a bulldog personality that reflected his six-feet-two, muscular build, dark complexion, and neatly trimmed beard. He had spent his childhood in El Paso, so he spoke fluent Spanish and was as tough as nails. Diplomacy and tact were completely foreign to him, and his boisterous voice could be heard across a football field—*during the game.*

I picked up the phone. "Hey, Art, what's up?"

"I just heard you have cancer."

"Yeah, breast cancer. Surgery's on Wednesday."

"Yeah, well, don't you die on me, you son of a bitch!" Then he hung up.

That's the guy version of a support system: quick, to the point, no BS, no hugging, no crying, and no extended conversations. A phone call twenty seconds long said it all—no elaboration necessary. I got the point and decided to try to follow his advice.

I spent my next thirty-six hours arranging call coverage for my patients and clearing my office schedule for two weeks. I was absolutely certain Marilyn had told me my recovery time would be two weeks, and I planned for that timeframe. The busy days made life bearable, but the nights were awful. The reality of my situation was settling in, and sleeping was almost impossible. Wednesday morning couldn't come soon enough, or so I thought.

Wednesday, June 17

My lump was to be injected with a radioactive isotope at 9:30 a.m. Surgery was to be at 2:00 p.m., so I needed to be at the hospital by 7:30 a.m. to register. On another beautiful, clear late-spring morning, Jenny, Julie, Jessica, and I left for Dallas. Although the weather was exhilarating, I was exhausted. The night before, all I could think about was the sentinel node, and how it really *had* to be negative. Negative meant cured. Then I could recover from surgery and end this nightmare. I was much too concerned about the lymph node to let any fear of surgery sneak in, but that changed when I walked into the hospital.

I identified myself at the registration desk at Zale Hospital, a private hospital adjacent to Parkland. The receptionist wrote down my last name, grinned, and handed me about one hundred pages of forms to complete. They contained the same damn thousand questions I'd answered last Thursday in Marilyn's office, only these were arranged in a slightly different order. It seemed as if the hospital and doctor weren't aware of each other's existence, and I felt like they were going out of their way to piss me off. But I was extremely anxious to get the surgery over, so I answered all of them again. Then I sat down with my family to wait.

At that time the Zale Hospital waiting room was huge. It was littered with dozens of green upholstered chairs arranged around large wooden planters filled with unidentifiable plants in various stages of dying. I never understood why hospitals considered dead plants to be an inspiration, but most seem to. If they can't keep a common houseplant green and vibrant, just how good can they be with live people?

Jenny, Julie, and Jessica were deep in conversation, and I tried to distract myself with dead plants and multipage forms, but my thoughts kept turning to the surgery. A surgeon's life is remarkably simple. I show up in the operating room; my patient is there, asleep, prepped, and ready to go. I only concerned myself with the cutting and sewing part. But now I was getting a taste of what my patients went through before entering the operating room, and I didn't like it.

Suddenly someone screamed "Johns" over the waiting room loudspeaker. We all jumped as if a firecracker had gone off under our chairs. The receptionist told me they were ready for me in Nuclear Medicine. I looked at Jenny and the kids and said, "Okay, here we go."

After taking a seat on a nondescript table in Nuclear Medicine, I took off my shirt. A moment later the radiology technician came in, introduced herself and said, "I need to inject the tumor."

Simple enough, but I began to wonder what the radioactive stuff would feel like when it shot out the end of that needle and spread into my chest. I didn't have to wait long to find out. It hurt like hell! Then the radiologist came in with another needle about the size of an ice pick that was attached to a syringe filled with blue fluid. I wondered why he was injecting the benign blue dye and had left the dangerous, radioactive stuff to be handled by the technician. Regardless, he didn't say much, just rammed the needle right in and pushed the plunger down. It was my first rush of pain for the day. Then they both left without asking me how I was.

"We'll call you back for the scan in about two hours," someone said as I put my shirt on.

Back in the waiting room, all I could think about was that one little stupid node. Everything was riding on it. I looked repeatedly at my watch. It was going to be a really long two hours.

I had just begun describing the events in Nuclear Medicine to the kids when "Dr. Johns, Dr. Delbert Johns" boomed over the loudspeaker.

I rarely used my first name. I was born two months after my mom's brother Delbert was killed in an auto accident. He had been a Navy pilot and had just returned from World War II. My parents decided to name me after him, Delbert Alan Johns. I always hated the name Delbert, so I went by Alan. I didn't want to go by D. Alan Johns, because that sounded like some snooty New England aristocrat. But on medical forms my name had to match my insurance card, ergo Delbert it was.

"Did you just hear 'Delbert Johns'?" I asked Jenny.

"Yep, somebody wants you."

I walked to the desk. "You have a call," the receptionist said, handing me the phone.

"This is Delbert Johns," I said, wondering what was up.

"Dr. Johns," a soft female voice said.

"Yes?"

"I'm Nasha, the surgery resident working with Dr. L."

"Okay." I was a little puzzled. "What can I do for you?"

"I need to do your H & P before we go to surgery."

A history and physical is the first step in the evaluation of every patient about to have surgery. Hospitals require it to be completed before taking any non-emergency patient to the operating room. I knew the rule but had forgotten about it. I also knew that nothing else was going to happen until the H and P was done.

"Great, let's get it done," I said.

Nasha came to the waiting room, introduced herself to us, and directed me to an exam room just down the hall and around the corner. I headed for the room while Nasha talked with Jenny and the kids. A small cubicle with dull yellow walls, the examination room sported an unidentifiable dead plant in the far right corner and a small exam table in the middle. A single chair sat near the door. I took it.

Nasha walked in. Young and slender, with a dark complexion, jet-black hair, and beautiful blue eyes, she wore the ubiquitous white doctor's coat with a stethoscope in the lower right pocket. Her assignment was to take my history, do a physical exam, record her findings, and assist during the surgery. Although she was no rookie, she seemed unusually nervous, probably because I was a doctor on the teaching faculty at her hospital. We spoke for a few moments, and I learned that she was a second-year surgery resident and had worked with Marilyn for the past three months. She was planning on doing a surgical oncology fellowship and specializing in the surgical treatment of breast cancer. She had never seen a male breast cancer patient and was very curious. As she began her questions, I was taken back twenty-five years.

Twenty-five years earlier, almost to the day, I had just started my third year of medical school and was about to do my very first H & P. The first two years of med school had been limited to classroom and laboratory work; students weren't exposed to living patients until the third year, when we learned to do history-and-physical examinations.

Before my third year, I'd watched the faculty, residents, and senior students do H & Ps, so all the questions were familiar, but I'd never actually confronted a patient, much less lain a hand on one. In order to gain experience, all third-year students were dispatched to unsuspecting patients' rooms in John Sealy Hospital. These patients had already suffered through this medical ritual at the hands of their *real* admitting doctor, as well as the fourth-, third-, and second-year residents, an intern, and a senior medical student. Third-year med students were the last to rehash the patients' misery in detail while subjecting every square inch of their bodies to one more intrusion. I really felt sorry for these folks, but there was no alternative—that was how the teaching system worked. If there weren't enough patients to go around, *two* teams of residents, interns, and students would be assigned the same patient, and the flood of questions and intrusion could quickly overwhelm.

Since third-year students usually had no idea which questions were important and which were completely superfluous, they asked all of them. The questioning might go on for hours. This was followed by the physical examination, which was largely a joke when performed by a third-year student. They had no clue what to look for and weren't even sure what they'd found when something seemed abnormal, so they'd poke and prod every nook and cranny of the patients' bodies, desperately hoping to find something.

I had been no different.

With some trepidation, I put on my doctor's coat and carefully placed my stethoscope in the left pocket and a reflex hammer, tuning fork (to test bone conduction hearing), and tape measure (just in case I needed to measure something) in the right pocket. I was primed and ready to diagnose any and every disease known to man.

My first H & P patient was on the fourth floor of John Sealy Hospital. When I reviewed the hospital chart before knocking on his door, I discovered he was a forty-four-year-old family doctor who had been practicing in Brownsville, Texas, for fourteen years. I also learned he was dying of leukemia and his treatment options had been exhausted. He had only a few weeks to live. He'd already undergone H & P exams by five members of my team before I arrived. The thought of asking him to endure another useless, pointless intrusion during his last few days on earth made me sick. But it was my assignment and I had no choice. I knocked on his door lightly, hoping he wouldn't hear. A soft, almost inaudible "Come in" answered my knock.

Dr. K had no family; he had been married to his profession. He was proud to have followed in the footsteps of his dad, who had been a family doctor. His leukemia had been diagnosed about two months earlier, and all treatment regimens had failed to slow its progression. Although gravely ill and in horrendous physical condition, he still had a sparkle in his eyes and an unmistakable zest for life.

I was in the middle of an apology and backing out the door when he lifted his head off the pillow, looked me straight in the eye, pointed to a dark corner of the room, and said, "Son, pull up that chair and sit down. We're going to do this and do it right."

During the next hour, he proceeded to teach me the nuances of obtaining a meaningful family, social, and medical history by asking and answering his own questions; he didn't skip a thing.

"You're going to be a doctor. That means never, ever take shortcuts. Your patients depend on you; don't let them down," he advised me.

When we finished the history, he struggled to sit up, obviously in pain, and directed me through the entire physical examination. He made sure I left nothing out. He noted every abnormality and what it meant. He wanted me to learn not only how to do a good history and physical examination, but also everything possible about his disease.

As miserable as he felt and as much pain as he was in, he patiently worked me through the entire process. About three hours later, I walked out of that dark, foreboding room with respect and enthusiasm for my profession that has endured to this day. Before leaving, I shook his hand, thanked him, and promised I wouldn't forget what he had done for me.

He died six days later.

I never forgot.

Fast-forward twenty-five years. When Nasha said to me, "I really don't need to do the whole physical. I'm sure you're in good shape," I responded with a silent grin. That simple statement suddenly and dramatically took my mind off what lay ahead.

I rose from my chair, sat on the exam table, looked her square in the eye, and began her lesson. "Nasha, it's *your* job to find out if I'm in good shape or not, and you've done nothing to determine that. You'll be the one in the OR with a scalpel, not me, so I'm depending on you. Besides, it's painfully obvious that I'm not a good judge of how I am, since I'm the idiot who waited three months to get something done."

She nodded as her eyes grew a little larger.

"It doesn't matter if I'm a doc and pissed off to be here. You do your job and do it right, every time. Never, ever take shortcuts with patients. We depend on you."

I could tell she was a little embarrassed, but she recovered nicely and, with my help, did an admirable and thorough job. When she finished, she put her stethoscope back in her lower right coat pocket and asked, "Are you okay, Dr. Johns?"

Unfortunately for her, I was losing my bravado and chose to be honest. "Shit, no, I'm not okay!" I replied, my voice cracking. "I've got cancer and I'm heading for the operating table. I'm scared to death." Her eyes widened again but she kept listening. "I'm terrified that I'll wake up to learn my nodes are positive and the cancer's spread. It's not the surgery, it's the idea of positive nodes that simply scares the shit out of me! I've avoided this for three damn months and I'm going to pay for that. And by the way, who is the damn anesthesiologist? Does he have any idea what the hell he's doing?"

Three months of fear, denial, frustration, repression, and anger finally spewed out. To her credit, Nasha just listened, knowing she need not answer. After I finished my rant, she took my hand.

"Dr. Johns, I promise I'll tell you about your nodes as soon as you wake up."

I felt better as I left the exam room. I guess my rant had been cathartic, even if it had been at Nasha's expense. I walked out to the waiting room recomposed and ready for the next step. "How'd it go?" Jenny asked.

"Pretty well." I wasn't lying.

For the next hour I sat slumped in my chair, imagining everything that could go wrong. The wait to get part of my body cut open had become another learning experience. I'd never really thought about the stress my patients felt, and being a surgeon made my own stress even worse. I thought of thousands of things that might not go well.

"It didn't go well" is a phrase we surgeons often use. We never say, "Something went wrong." It's always, "It didn't go well." I had already decided never to use that term again.

While going through my mental disaster list, I was interrupted by "Dr. Johns, Dr. Delbert Johns" once again. They were ready for me in Nuclear Medicine. A nice technician directed me to the Nuclear Medicine scanner suite, where a huge metal table occupied the center of the dark room. Above the table was a machine that resembled the warp drive on the Starship Enterprise. It was a massive, plastic ovoid that looked like it might fall from the ceiling at any time, unmercifully crushing whatever lay beneath, and in a few moments that would be me.

"Take off your shirt, Dr. Johns, and lie down on the table," the tech ordered.

The table was cold. I glanced up expecting to see a green, radioactive death ray coming straight at me. Instead, the entire mechanism moved back and forth over my chest, making a strange sound like a washing machine struggling through its spin cycle with a slightly unbalanced load. Sooner than I expected, it was over and a black indelible "X" marked the spot on my chest.

"Thanks, that's it. You can go back to the waiting room. They'll call when surgery is ready for you," the tech explained.

Then the *really* hard part began: waiting my turn for the OR. That's where my family came in handy. After coming back from Nuclear Medicine, I began feeling sorry for myself, but Jenny, Jessica, and Julie would have none of that. They just kept talking. In reality, I'm sure they were more scared than I was, but they were determined to get me through this. Families are good.

Before long a door opened into the waiting room and in walked Nurse R. "Dr. Johns, Dr. Delbert Johns," she shouted. I quickly looked around the room just in case there was another Dr. Delbert

Johns waiting to have his tit cut off. Finding none, I raised my hand. Almost simultaneously, Julie and Jessica said, "Daddy, that nurse wants you."

No shit, I thought.

The nurse directed Jenny and me to a small, sterile-looking room. In the center of the room sat a stretcher covered with a white sheet, a yellowing blanket neatly folded at one end and a nicely fluffed pillow on the other. A stainless-steel IV pole stood guard on the left side with a plump one-liter bag of normal saline hanging from one prong. The scene reminded me of the death chamber at the Texas State Penitentiary in Huntsville.

I could almost hear the pillow say, "Come on, Dr. Johns, lie down and relax—this won't hurt a bit." I was terrified—a grown man and a surgeon, scared like a little kid at a horror show. Like a wildcat caught in a trap, I had an uncontrollable urge to run like hell, go home, and hope it would all go away. I still get nervous and sweaty thinking about that room.

I stood trancelike.

"You should get undressed and put on the stupid hospital gown," Jenny said. "You know, the one that lets your ass fall out the back."

I turned and looked at her. Her common sense and humor always lighten the mood when things get tense. She was right. Hospital gowns weren't at all practical; doctors almost never need access to a patient's ass. All the stuff we need to examine (heart, lungs, throat, eyes, ears, breasts, abdomen, arms, etc.) aren't anywhere near the ass. Why would someone design a gown that opens to an anatomic area docs care nothing about and usually try to avoid?

But it was clothes off, gown on, ass out.

Next a nurse sauntered in, needle in hand, and connected me to the bottle of saline hanging next to the death stretcher. The big show was getting nearer and nearer.

I was practically naked, ass hanging out, with an IV in my left arm. Fortunately, Jenny was amazingly strong and resilient, refusing to let me get overly worried or serious, although I'm sure she was terrified as well. I was about to throw up when another resident walked in.

"Hello, Dr. Johns, I'm Dr. Blah Blah," he muttered. "How are you doing?" I have no idea what his name was.

Well, dumb shit, I've got cancer and I'm about to have my chest cut off in hopes that it hasn't already spread to my liver, spine, and brain. How the hell do you think I'm doing?

"I'm just fine," I lied.

With that he started his canned informed-consent discussion that he'd regurgitated a hundred times. "You realize, Dr. Johns, we aren't perfect and you might die. And if you do, it won't be our fault. The drugs we utilize have side effects, like blah, blah, blah. You also might experience blah, blah, and blah."

I could take no more. "I understand you need to say all that crap," I interrupted, "but would you please skip it and ask the anesthesiologist to come in."

He stopped, a little annoyed that I had broken into his speech. "Sure." Then he left the room.

"Don't be an ass!" Jenny scolded me like I were a kid who had just talked back to his teacher.

A few minutes later, the anesthesiologist, known among surgeons as the gas passer, walked in. "Dr. Johns, how are you doing?" he asked as he sat down next to the stretcher.

I couldn't believe it. Every doc was asking the same idiotic question. *Well, dumb shit number four, I'm scared as hell; hope you're having a good day, too.*

"Fine" I told him, sparing him the truth.

I knew exactly what was about to happen; I knew about

anesthesia, intubation, and ventilation during surgery. I knew what might happen, could happen, and probably would happen. I was also at my breaking point, and I knew it. Fortunately, I also knew about a drug called Versed. It's an amnesic. I wouldn't remember anything after it went in my vein. It's a great drug, and I wanted some immediately.

Before Dr. Blah number two could say another word, I asked if he would skip all the informed-consent crap and please get me a big slug of Versed. He looked a little shocked, but Jenny intervened.

"I'm not telling you how to do your job, but I'd suggest giving it to him now. Otherwise we might have to chase him down the hall to get this done. I doubt you want to see his butt hanging out of that gown as he runs out the door, dragging the IV with him," she said.

Dr. Blah agreed, and about a minute later, a nice dose of Versed was on its way into my vein. Like an addict salivating over his next narcotic hit, I lay there, absolutely scared out of my mind, waiting for the drug to do what it was supposed to do.

Damn, I feel nothing, I thought. *When in the hell is this stuff going to work? It's probably out of date, and the damn doctor didn't check the expiration!*

I turned to Jenny and said, "This shit isn't working. I need some more."

The next memory I have is of waking up in the recovery room.

CHAPTER FIFTEEN

Drains

According to Jessica and Julie, after the Versed hit, I was laughing and joking with everyone within earshot, right up to the time the nurse wheeled me out of the room. Then I waved and laughed at people as I was rolled down the hallway into the operating room.

I love pharmacology!

The next thing I recall was desperately trying to open my eyes. I felt as if I'd awakened in the middle of the night in an unfamiliar hotel room. I didn't know where I was, which side of the bed to get out of, or where the bathroom was. Gobs of anesthetic gas and a five-hour operation had me groggy and confused.

As my mind cleared a bit, I remembered that I was about to have surgery. *Wow,* I thought, *the Versed finally hit.* More thoughts lumbered through my mind: *Damn, they haven't started the operation! I need another slug of Versed. Where the hell are Jenny and that damn anesthesiologist?*

Then my vision cleared a bit. The room was darker than I remembered. It was a lot bigger, and a dingy yellow curtain that hadn't been there before hung to my left. Someone moaned on the other side of the curtain. I glanced up at my IV and noticed there were *two* bags hanging up there, both dripping liquids into my vein.

What in the hell is going on? I thought. *And who put up these stupid guardrails?*

I began to turn to my right to ask Jenny to get the anesthesiologist. That was a DBM (damn big mistake). It felt as if I'd rolled directly onto a dozen red-hot, six-inch ice picks stuck firmly into a block of cement, points up, each one embedding into the right side of my chest.

The pain was my first clue that my five-hour surgery was over, and that realization reversed the anesthesia and narcotic effects instantly. Frantically, I reached across with my left hand, trying to feel through the bandages for a big incision in my right armpit. If an incision was there, the sentinel node was positive, the tumor had spread, and they had done an axillary node dissection. But every time I reached for my right side, the pain stopped me.

Tears had filled my eyes, and I had clinched my teeth to prepare for another attempt to feel for the incision, when a vaguely familiar voice floated to me from the foot of my bed. I opened my eyes and saw Nasha in her bloody scrubs, surgical cap still covering her hair and mask tied loosely around her neck.

"Dr. Johns, your nodes are negative." It was ten-thirty at night. She had kept her word and patiently waited an hour until I was conscious enough to understand what she was saying.

Your nodes are negative are the four most beautiful words I have ever heard.

Smiling, she walked closer so she could check the surgical dressing. I was so excited, so relieved, and so thankful that I laughed and tried rolling over to give her a big hug, but the ice picks hit again and I threw up on her instead.

She didn't seem to mind, though. She helped my nurse get us

both cleaned up and left with a sincere, "Good night, and thanks for the great advice."

And that's when I began to cry. My nodes being negative overwhelmed me, and pent-up emotion and nerves flooded me. I wouldn't need chemo or radiation. Because of my procrastination, the cancer easily could have spread to my lungs, liver, or brain, but it hadn't. Despite being a complete idiot, I was going to survive.

Now I could continue my life and not have to worry about fighting cancer or dying. I repeated those two words, *negative nodes*, over and over. I felt very lucky; life had shot a bullet at me and I'd dodged it.

A few moments later my nurse peeked through the opening in the curtains surrounding my stretcher. "How you doing, Dr. Johns? Ready to go to your room?"

"Damn, I'm great! Let's go!" I was still loopy from the drugs. Off we went, me lying on my left side, smiling like I'd just won the lottery, sheet thrown off and dragging on the floor, ass hanging out the back of my gown. I greeted everyone I saw on that short trip to my room with a wink and "Hey, how you doing? Negative nodes!"

I'd been assigned a suite on the sixth floor of Zale Hospital in exchange for a small, up-front fee. It featured a separate bedroom for family members, a nice TV, and two large windows that overlooked the hospital entrance and parking lot. Jenny had opened both windows to let in the spring air, and she and the kids were waiting when I rolled in. I was still absolutely ecstatic and overflowing with relief. I had the urge to run over and hug them, but this time I remembered the pain and stayed put.

Suddenly the door to the suite opened and our good friends Gaye and Bill walked in. Gaye and Jenny had taught together at the Shriners burn hospital in Galveston, and we'd all remained good friends over the years. The day before, Bill, an internist, had driven up from Houston so he and Gaye could be with Jenny while I was in surgery. Later I found out there'd been an entire contingent of friends from Fort Worth in the waiting room while Marilyn worked on me. According to Jenny, all they needed was a keg of beer and a band and it would have been a real party. Good friends really are priceless.

Bill released the side rail on the right side of my bed and helped me out. It was bathroom time. Steadying me with his left hand, he kept patting me on the back with his right, saying how happy he was that I was going to be okay. I was so touched by his friendship that I threw up all over his boots. He cleaned up the mess, got me back into bed, and I promptly passed out. I slept really well for the first time in months.

Post-op, Day One

Julie, my oldest daughter, was having a particularly memorable time. She had spent her twenty-second birthday at the hospital with her mom and sister, hoping like hell Daddy wouldn't die while getting his breast cut off. To make her life even better, the next morning she got a speeding ticket while driving back to the hospital. She tried the old "my dad's in the hospital for cancer surgery" excuse, but the officer didn't buy it. She arrived at the hospital more than a little chagrined.

My morning, on the other hand, was spectacular. I awakened feeling wonderful. Despite being less than twenty-four hours out from surgery, I felt no pain and began thinking this wasn't going to be too bad after all. Breakfast had been placed on a tray next to my bed, and especially for hospital food, it smelled pretty good. I began to formulate my plan: I'd get out of bed, eat breakfast, and get the hell home.

I took a breath, rolled to my right, and tried to put my feet on the floor. I was instantly reminded what had taken place the day before and why I was in the hospital.

Julie helped me out of bed, maneuvered me into the bathroom in front of the mirror, and removed the bandage so I could see Marilyn's handiwork. An incision ran transversely across the entire right side of my chest, from armpit to sternum—no muscle or nipple remained. The area was concave, like it had been crushed with a big rock. There were a couple of three-foot-long, clear plastic tubes snaking from underneath my skin and emptying into two plastic bulbs held by a Velcro belt around my waist.

These little gadgets are known as drains (we surgeons are really clever with names). The tubing is flexible and small, about a quarter-inch in diameter. One end is placed through the skin and directly into the middle of the surgical wound. That end is perforated to let fluid seep into the tube. The opposite end of the tubing is brought out through a small puncture wound a few inches beneath the surgical incision line and attached to a collapsible bulb. The bulb sucks blood, pus, and other excretions from beneath the skin. This stuff "weeps" from the large, raw area where muscle, connective tissue, fat, tendons, and various other body tissues used to reside. Without drains, this mess would keep collecting under the skin until it got infected or erupted through the skin like an oil-field gusher.

I looked in the mirror again and noticed I was the proud owner of not one, but *two* of these damn drains. They reminded me of the dual exhaust pipes we proudly added to our '57 Chevys in high school.

Finally Julie helped me back to bed just as a cheerful nurse walked in. She greeted me with, "Good morning, Dr. Johns! How are we this beautiful morning?"

I looked up and thought, *What the hell do you want, Little Miss Cheerful?* I didn't need a weather report; I was busy trying to figure out when and how I could get my drains out, but I said, "I'm doing great, how are you?"

"You saw the drains?" she inquired.

Hospitals are full of dumb questions. How could I miss two garden hoses coming out of my chest, connected to two plastic jars of bloody gunk hanging around my waist? "Yeah, I noticed."

"I'm your drain consultant," she said as she began to inspect the gunk-filled containers.

Charming title. I knew about lactation consultants, but this was my first encounter with a drain consultant.

"We need to teach you proper care of your new drains, how to empty the containers, and how to hook them back up again." Her speech reminded me of my mammogram experience. No telling what hell she was about to put me through in the name of education.

"Thanks, but I'm a surgeon, and I know all about drains," I said, hoping to avoid whatever she had in mind.

"Don't be an ass!" Jenny said. She gave me a fake smile, then turned to our new drain consultant. "You'd better show us what to do, because I'm the one who will be doing it." She pointed to me. "He may be a surgeon, but when it comes to his own health, he's a wimp!"

The two of them conspired, forcing me to get educated. The drain jugs were to be emptied every four hours, around the clock, and the volume of stuff coming out of each drain dutifully recorded along with the time and date. Unfortunately, I knew that doctors rarely pay much attention to information we ask patients to observe and record. The information is usually marginally important. The real purpose is to give our patients "important" tasks so they can be in charge of *something*. Usually this helps take their focus away from what we have done to them. But I figured that mentioning that fact to Jenny and Nurse Drain Consultant would just piss off both of them, so I kept my mouth shut.

The lesson required a full hour for me to become "drain-educated." Satisfied that my education was complete, the nurse left, leaving behind a dozen forms on which I was to record all that useless information.

I wasn't hurting, didn't need anything else for pain, and was bored as hell, nervously pacing back and forth from bed to window. Even though my room was four times larger than a normal hospital room, it felt like a doghouse: confining and claustrophobic.

I walked over to Jenny and the kids and said, "Well, that was fun. Now it's time to go home." Realizing that "home" meant they, not the nurses, would be responsible for taking care of me, they weren't thrilled, but they figured it was better than listening to me whine.

There was only one slight problem. Marilyn had not done her morning rounds, and she was solely responsible for discharging me from the hospital. Like most surgeons, she hated hospital rounds and made them only when the mood struck or she had absolutely nothing left to do. I'd always made early-morning rounds, but that was more because of my normal routine. It definitely was not the norm. I'd always gotten up at five, exercised, and was at the hospital by seven to see my hospitalized patients. I was learning firsthand how impatient one can get while waiting on a doctor.

I asked my nurse when Dr. L would be gracing us with her presence; she laughed and said, "Sometime later, maybe even today."

I wanted to go home, and I'd had just enough narcotics to let my naturally warped personality emerge. I was bored, and when I'm bored I begin to scheme. Plus I was totally high on life. I was cured, the surgery was finished, and the entire ordeal was almost over. Finding a way to get out of the hospital became my challenge of the day, and I figured that I would need to facilitate my own dismissal.

As I glanced at the open window that looked out on Zale's main entrance, I hatched a plan. I had watched folks walk in and out of the hospital all morning. Zale was a state-of-the-art private hospital, very classy and uptown, catering to Dallas's snooty elite. I was still dressed in my flower-covered designer hospital gown with three tiny strings holding the back partially shut. My bare butt peeked out beneath the third string.

With a nice dose of drugs still coursing through my veins, I took a seat in the window, butt facing outward. I figured the folks walking from their cars to the hospital wouldn't expect a bare ass facing them several floors above the otherwise classy front entrance. I sat in that open window for several minutes, enjoying the morning breeze after my brush with death.

Just as I had figured, it didn't take long before a nurse roared into the room to "check my vital signs." I grinned and told her my butt was cold, but the rest of my vitals were fine. It wasn't long before Marilyn showed up and signed my discharge papers. Jenny apologized, but Marilyn wasn't particularly amused. Both ladies figured something like this was bound to happen, they just didn't know when.

A half-hour later we were on the way home, and the feeling of relief was indescribable, drains and all. Little did I know that the worst five months of my life lay directly ahead.

CHAPTER SIXTEEN

Recovery

I loved doing surgery but never gave much thought to how my patients felt after I dug around in their abdomens for a few hours, shook their hands, and dismissed them from the hospital with a glib "See you in two weeks." It wasn't that I didn't care (I did), but as a busy surgeon, I was eager to move on to my next surgical challenge. Now I was getting firsthand experience with what postsurgical hell was all about.

My two drains reminded me of an alien struggling to crawl out of my chest, one small finger at a time. To prevent the tubes from falling out, each one had been firmly secured to my skin with black silk sutures that felt like they were the size of a rope. The garden-hose tubes and collection bottles incessantly became entangled in everything around me. It was a constant challenge to walk from one room to another without yanking on one of them. Worse than that, the drains were a continuous reminder that I had cancer.

I quickly became fed up with the tedious job of emptying the surgical drains every four hours and dutifully recording the amount of goop they had sucked out. More than that, the drains and bulbs were the ultimate invasion of my body, and for some reason I couldn't tolerate that feeling.

I carried on with this routine for six days. I understood Marilyn's rationale: She wanted to know how much fluid/blood/pus was draining from beneath the skin and at what rate. But those numbers didn't really affect my recovery. The drains were supposed to stay in until the drainage stopped to ensure that the fluids wouldn't collect under the skin. But I had no use for them, even though Jenny was determined I would follow Marilyn's orders.

Worse than those alien drains coming out of my chest was the fact that I had to lie flat on my back to sleep, and I hadn't done that in thirty years. Searing pain met every attempt I made to change position, a reminder that a chunk of my chest was gone. I quickly learned which way I could move without screaming, but that didn't help a much more disturbing sensation.

Most everyone has awakened in the middle of the night and discovered that their arm has fallen asleep and become completely numb and paralyzed. This phenomenon results from pressure on the nerve bundles going to the arm through the neck. In layman's terms, pressure disables the nerves and "detaches" the arm from the brain.

A mastectomy does the same thing to the chest. Although most of the skin overlying my chest had been preserved, everything underneath was removed, including all of the cutaneous (skin) nerves. The skin on my chest was effectively "disconnected" from my brain.

Because of this, by my third post-operative day the right side of my chest felt like Dr. L had stapled a piece of plywood to it— the whole area was completely numb. The entire area felt as if it belonged to someone else. The combination of numb skin on top of bloody muscle and bone created an absolutely bizarre sensation.

I had been told that the feeling in that area would return when my nerves grew back, but by now I was a little skeptical.

Docs (myself included) tend to think of some problems as minimal (which, in the big scheme of things, they are). We're not dishonest; we just tend to focus on the "big picture." Yet these same "little" problems can be very troublesome and problematic for our patients. When things aren't progressing as expected, patients need someone to blame, and their doctors are good first targets. To make things even worse, patients often hear something that is drastically different than what their doctors have actually said. I was beginning to understand how this well-known phenomenon happens. I'm certain that Marilyn told me about the numbness, but all I heard was "mastectomy" and "cancer"—nothing else registered.

With some effort and a lot of pain, I could move my right arm. Trying to *control* my arm and hand, however, was a different story. The combination of a numb chest and a very painful pectoralis muscle made purposeful movement of my right arm almost impossible. I found shaving, combing my hair, brushing my teeth, getting dressed, and eating to be problematic. On a more personal note, hitting my target when I emptied my bladder was even more challenging. Aiming with a bum right arm (I never was very adept with my left) was, at best, difficult. I either completely missed, covering the floor like a little boy being toilet trained, or hit the drain bottles hanging down from my waist, sending urine splattering all over the bathroom walls.

To make matters worse, by the fourth day after surgery I was incredibly bored. I'd gone from my hyperspeed career to slogging around the house, trying to find *anything* meaningful to do. All I accomplished, however, was to drive Jenny and my daughters crazy.

If I could have ignored those damn drains, slept on my stomach, rolled over without crying, and hit the toilet even half the time, I could have dealt with the boredom. The only thing that made life tolerable was knowing that my journey with the lump was over—I didn't need any more treatment.

Jenny and the kids had been patient with me, but only to a point. The "I had cancer surgery last week" excuse quickly lost its impact. By post-op day five, the family decided I needed to resume some of my daily exercise routine (translation: get out of the house and away from them for a while). So Jenny dropped me off at the fitness center and said she'd be back in a couple of hours.

I climbed onto an exercise bike and took off like there was no tomorrow. It felt great to sweat from exercise instead of terror. But the drains continued to drive me nuts, and the next day, I decided they had to come out. I just needed a plan. Since I hadn't received permission from Dr. L to remove them, there was no possibility that Jenny would agree to help me take them out, so I did the logical thing: I waited until she left the house. As her car pulled out of the driveway, I called Gerry, a friend and a fellow OB-GYN who lived a few blocks away, and asked him to come over. I didn't tell him why.

Gerry was a few years younger than I, and we'd been in the same practice for several years. He has a prematurely receding hairline, wears wire-rimmed glasses, and is very meticulous and deliberate by nature. I figured he'd need a little encouragement to help me take the drains out, so after he rang our doorbell and I invited him in, I gave him a beer before going into detail about what I needed him to do. Sure enough, since he never had removed post-mastectomy drains in his medical career, he was a little reluctant to pull out mine.

I explained how desperate I was, promised him another beer, then cut the sutures holding the drains in place before he could say no. He gradually warmed to the idea and finally agreed to help me. I told him, "Grab the first one, start pulling, and for God's sake, don't stop until it's out."

I had been under anesthesia when the drains were put in, but unfortunately I was not when Gerry began pulling. He grabbed the end of the first tube with both hands, grinned, then ran toward the back door. The scene reminded me of pulling a tooth with a string tied to a doorknob—once the door is pushed, there's no going back.

When Gerry yanked out the first drain, it felt like a rottweiler had grabbed the end of a garden hose that happened to be anchored under my skin with barbed fishing hooks, then had taken off after a squirrel. I felt "a little pressure," as we doctors love to say.

Taking out the first drain turned out to be a bit more painful than I had anticipated, so I can't believe I let Gerry pull the second one out, but I did. When my vision cleared, both drains were lying on the floor, and the couch and floor were splattered with a thin, bloody fluid.

As soon as my voice returned, I thanked Gerry and gave him another beer, and he left. I considered calling Dr. L to let her know what I'd done, but I thought better of it. I certainly would (and did) catch enough hell from Jenny to compensate for anything Dr. L would have said. My relief was palpable, though; now I could begin my recovery process in earnest. The drains had been such a psychological barrier for me that I figured I would just have to cope with the fluid if it built up under my skin. I also knew that any buildup could be easily drained with a syringe and needle, and the idea of that procedure bothered me a lot less than the drains.

Five days later, Jenny and I went to Dallas for my follow-up appointment with Marilyn L, who thought she would be removing my drains. I was feeling much better, both physically and mentally. The past few months of fear and angst were abating; the cancer was gone, surgery was over, and I was looking forward to resuming my life. Although my "plywood" chest was a constant reminder of what had happened, I figured that would also fade with time.

As Jenny and I waited in the exam room, she mentioned how great it would be when Dr. L gave me the go-ahead to go back to work and get out of her hair. I agreed with her, stood, and walked over to the window with a huge smile on my face. The white, fluffy clouds that accented the blue Texas sky made me happy to be alive; it was one of those rare moments of pure ebullience. My nodes were negative, I was past the surgery, and I could see my life getting back to normal very soon.

Sixty seconds later, that all changed.

The door opened and Dr. L, somber and serious as usual, walked in. Her attention was immediately drawn to where the drain bulbs should have been. She asked what happened to them, and in the midst of my story about them falling out while I was asleep, Jenny interrupted, "The idiot took them out with a little help from one of his friends."

Dr. L seemed slightly pissed but not surprised. I managed a sheepish grin. Having a surgeon for a patient had probably been one of the great challenges of her professional life.

Off came my shirt and Dr. L checked the incision, which looked fine except for a small collection of fluid under the skin. She explained she would remove the fluid with a syringe and needle. Growling something barely audible about a dumb-ass doctor, she walked to the door to get what she needed. As she gripped the door handle she stopped, turned, and said, "I'll be back in a minute, and we'll talk about your chemotherapy."

The word stopped me cold. Not since I first discovered the lump had I felt blood rush from my head with such a vengeance. My bravado and optimism collapsed in a nanosecond. Marilyn walked out the door and I turned to Jenny.

"Chemotherapy?" I shouted. I stood up and walked back to the window. "What in the hell is she talking about? That's total bullshit! My nodes were negative, the cancer's gone. Why the hell does she want to talk about chemotherapy? People with *cancer* get chemotherapy. I don't have cancer anymore." Then I began shaking uncontrollably.

Jenny came over and put her arm around me as I looked out the same window that had given me such comfort just a few moments ago. Stunned, I began to sob. What the hell was going on?

Dr. L came back into the room, syringe and needle in hand. Sensing that something was amiss, she laid them on a nearby counter. "What's wrong?"

"You said 'chemotherapy' a minute ago," I blurted. "Have you forgotten about my negative nodes?"

She shook her head and explained that she hadn't forgotten. Then she gave me that "knowing doctor" look, the same one I had used with my patients a thousand times. The look means *just be quiet and listen to me, because I know what's best for you.*

"Sit down; we need to talk," she said.

Numb all over, I did as I was told. She said that the final pathology report was back. She shuffled through my paperwork, found it, and took it out of the file.

I continued to shake.

She explained that when my tumor parameters were taken into consideration, chemotherapy would improve my chances of surviving for five years from 85 percent to 95 percent.

Survive? Damn! She clearly said survive, not cure. The word "survival" really struck me. "Survival" carries a lot of negative connotations, and it has become yet another word I never use with patients.

For the second time in five minutes, one simple word was both unexpected and devastating, and I stopped listening. Now she was talking about survival, not cure. To be fair, I don't remember any of my doctors ever discussing cure. I'd just assumed that was what the mastectomy and negative nodes were all about. I'd also assumed that if I had negative nodes, I wouldn't need chemotherapy or any other treatment. I was an OB-GYN specialist, not a cancer specialist, so all this was a bit foreign to me.

Welcome, Alan, to the world of cancer terminology, where they never talk cure, they talk survival, two vastly different words with completely different implications.

Patients think cure, and at that moment I was very much a patient. I had planned to have the cancer cut out, move on, and die of something else many years later.

I was speechless.

Dr. L realized I needed time to digest what she had said, so she turned her attention to the fluid under my incision. I never saw the syringe she used, and I never felt the needle go through my skin. My mind was on one thing: chemotherapy.

When she finished, she said, "I'll get rid of this syringe and be back in a minute." Then she was out the door.

Red-eyed and mumbling incoherently, I looked at Jenny. She gently nudged me back to reality, as she had done so many times in our twenty-eight years of marriage. "Ninety-five percent is a hell of a lot better than eighty-five percent," she said, rather matter-of-factly. "I'm a teacher, I know these things." As I put on my shirt, she continued, "You've had five minutes to feel sorry for yourself, so let's get on to the next step. You've already done the hard part." Her bravado was beginning to crack, though.

Realizing she was right, I composed myself as Dr. L walked back in. Before she could say anything, I rolled up my sleeve, presented my arm, and said, "Let's get started." She didn't even flinch—nothing I did surprised her anymore.

"You have an appointment with our oncologist next Monday," she said. "He'll discuss your options."

Options? I thought. I don't want options; I want to get this crap over with.

Before I could say anything, Jenny chimed in, "We'll be there, thanks."

I walked out of the office almost as devastated as when I'd left the pathology department at Harris Methodist Hospital a mere four weeks earlier. If Jenny hadn't been there, I might have kept on walking, maybe to Florida.

CHAPTER SEVENTEEN

July 6, 1998: The Oncologist

On Monday morning Jenny and I drove back to Dallas to meet with Dr. M, an oncologist who was a faculty member at the University of Texas Southwestern Medical Center, and whom Marilyn had recommended. We were escorted into his office and met by a portly gentleman dressed in an antiquated checked shirt with no tie, wrinkled khaki slacks, and black lace-up shoes. Dr. M was in his early sixties with thinning, curly gray hair that looked as if he hadn't combed it in weeks. His thick, black-rimmed bifocals rested halfway down his nose, making him look like an absentminded professor.

After proper introductions, Jenny, Dr. M, and I sat around a circular conference table in his office. My operative and pathology reports lay to his right; his coffee cup rested next to two white legal pads positioned between us.

"You need chemotherapy," he said, answering my first question before I could ask it. Small talk obviously wasn't his forte. "It'll improve your five-year survival [chances] by 10 percent. The real issue is to determine the medicines we should use." He clasped his hands.

I found it interesting that he used the word *medicines*; it sounded so much better than *chemotherapy*. I drew in a deep breath, and for the next thirty minutes, Dr. M reviewed statistics on the various combinations of "medicines" that could be used. He reviewed the intervals between doses and the blood tests that would be necessary to monitor their effects. These protocols, as he euphemistically referred to them, had different effects on different tumors, and his recommendations were based on the specific parameters of my tumor, combined with the individual therapeutic characteristics of each chemotherapeutic drug (or medicine, as he continued to call them). He finished our discussion by explaining the potential side effects of his medicines. There were more than a few.

As much as I wanted to ignore the possibility, Dr. M made it clear that there was a 15 percent chance the cancer might recur and kill me if I didn't agree to the chemotherapy. I hadn't planned on any of this, but I knew I had to warm to the idea of chemotherapy if I wanted to increase my odds at life by 10 percentage points.

After what seemed like a month of detailed explanations, Dr. M gave Jenny and me his suggested protocol. I would be given six doses of chemotherapy, one every three weeks. I would receive two different medicines: Adriamycin and Cytoxan. Both would be administered intravenously, and the protocol needed to start in two or three weeks—as soon as I had sufficiently recovered from surgery.

I knew a bit about both drugs, and I had always wondered who came up with a name like Cytoxan, which sounds both ominous and dangerous. Adriamycin, on the other hand, sounds like a friendly, quaint little town in France. The pharmaceutical industry's logic had always escaped me.

Finally Dr. M tore his notes off the legal pad and handed them to me. I felt like a felon being given his paperwork by the judge who'd just sentenced him to four months in jail and said, "Here, read this while you're doing time." I guess he wanted me to study what he had written, but after taking a quick glance, I realized I couldn't read his notes any better than I could read my own. I carefully folded the paper and put it in my pocket.

Quite proud of himself, he smiled and removed his glasses. "Any questions?"

Yeah, I thought, would you mind translating your notes into English? "No questions," I said instead. "I've got a lot to think about." I wasn't particularly afraid of the chemo, but this entire process was a constant reminder that we were talking *survival* instead of *cure*.

"I'll send you back to Dr. L. She'll get you on the surgery schedule to have a portacath put in."

His last three words hit me hard. The portacath was another thing I hadn't thought about.

"Portacath?" I said, almost out of breath, as if I'd just been sucker punched. I managed to take a deep breath. A portacath is a ten-inch plastic tube with a spherical silicone reservoir on one end. The entire gadget is inserted beneath the skin below the collarbone. The catheter would be inserted through an incision there and directly into my superior vena cava, which empties into the right atrium of my heart. After that, my skin would be sewn shut over the reservoir, and the entire contraption would lie hidden beneath the skin, providing a way to get medicine into my venous circulation quickly and efficiently without having to start an intravenous line. Once inserted, a portacath usually stays in place for years.

Nope, no thanks. I had no desire for another surgery. Furthermore, portacaths are used for *really* sick patients who need frequent large doses of intravenous drugs, and I didn't want to be counted among that group. Considering how well I had tolerated those damn drains, I knew this thing would drive me nuts.

I thanked Dr. M and told him I'd make the appointment with

Dr. L myself, though I had no intention of doing so. I just wanted out of his office; I didn't want to think about chemotherapy, and I definitely didn't want to worry about another surgery.

The reality of needing chemotherapy was sinking in, and I was close to freaking out. My experience with chemotherapy had been limited to a four-week rotation during my senior year of medical school in Galveston. I was assigned to a chemotherapy ward where patients terminally ill with advanced cancer were treated. Many had metastatic melanoma and were receiving the really toxic stuff. That's where I learned how nasty chemo drugs are.

During that rotation, I'd be assigned to a patient. After taking his history, I'd start an IV, then someone would hand me a fifty-cubic-centimeter syringe full of "medicine." Before I could inject a single drop, however, the head nurse always warned me that the chemo would eat a hole in the patient's arm if it leaked out of the vein and into the surrounding tissue. With that grisly picture in mind, it often took me an hour to get that little syringe of meds pushed in.

Before finishing the rotation, I saw two patients whose IVs had infiltrated, allowing their "medicines" to leak into the muscles in their arms. Their forearms looked like they'd been excavated with a dull dinner fork: Ulcerative craters, four inches wide and one and a half inches deep, had appeared. These cavernous holes took months to heal, if they ever did.

Portacaths had been developed primarily to negate that risk. But I couldn't stand the idea of one in my body. I have fat, juicy, ready-to-be-stuck veins in both arms. The chances of leakage should be minimal, and I didn't want to go through surgery for the portacath only to have yet another procedure to take the damn thing out months later.

Again, no thanks.

By the time we arrived home, I had deciphered Dr. M's shorthand enough to understand the regimen he was suggesting. Jenny and I put on some country music, poured drinks, and went out by the pool to talk. I brought up Dr. N., a friend in Fort Worth who was an oncologist, and told Jenny I wanted to see him for a second opinion. She agreed it was a good idea. I figured that poison was poison, whether it was administered east or west of the Trinity River. Dallas's poison couldn't be better than Fort Worth's, and ours was closer to home.

Two days later, Jenny and I sat in front of Dr. N, a man about my age, five feet seven, and bald with a graying mustache. For the years I've known him, he's always worn a tie with his white shirt and knee-length doctor's coat. Unlike most oncologists, he's a happy fellow, with a dry sense of humor that's most evident when he's playing golf—where he can make his own rules. One of his favorites is what he calls a tracer putt. He drops a golf ball on the green and kicks it toward the hole to determine its speed and break. Using that information, he hardly ever missed a putt. Dr. N figured that compared with the cancer with which he dealt every day, the rules of golf weren't all that important.

"Alan, I'm really sorry you're here," were his first words, and immediately I understood that Dr. N *got it*. He knew what I was going through, and his acknowledgment of my predicament was a great way to start.

I handed him my pathology report along with the Dallas protocol, both of which he digested in a few minutes. With no hesitation, he said, "Alan, you need to do this."

With his opinion confirming what I had already been told, my decision was made. I didn't need any questions, options, notes, or statistics to mull over.

"What's next?" I asked, anxious to move on.

"First, let's go over a few of the side effects," he said. He told me I'd lose my hair and that the poison could permanently damage my heart muscle and lungs. My white blood cell count would drop, making me more susceptible to infections. Bladder damage might cause me to pee blood for a while. I would probably get a *little* nauseated, and I would definitely be tired.

I shook my head. For all that, *hopefully* any remaining cancer cells would be killed, too. Chemotherapy wasn't going to be fun, but it was certainly preferable to death.

We agreed that Fridays would be my day. That gave me the weekend to recover so I could be back at work on Monday. Since I was having chemotherapy, not surgery, I figured 48 hours would be plenty of time to recover. Other than the heart, lungs, stomach, and bladder stuff, it didn't sound too bad.

Agreeing that I had "pretty good veins for a doctor, Dr. N suggested I go to the "infusion room" and make certain the nurses thought my veins were big enough for my first dose on Friday. I liked the term "infusion room"; it sounded better than "poisoning room" or "chemotherapy room" or "you've-got-cancer-and-are-going-to-die room." *Infusion* had a really nice sterile, clinical, and benign ring to it.

Dr. N pointed across the waiting room to a large entryway with "Infusion Room" carefully painted in gold block letters above the door. Jenny and I walked over to the forty-foot by fifty-foot room and peeked in. Recliners were lined up side-by-side along three walls, five on each side, all facing toward the center. Seven-foot, stainless-steel IV poles stood guard beside each recliner. A row of short windows lined the east wall near the ceiling, allowing sunlight to hit the IV poles and create a bizarre, almost ominous pattern of shadows on the tile floor. The nurses' desks and pharmacy occupied the fourth wall.

Soft, soothing music played in the background. The room had a very distinctive and unpleasant medicinal smell that burned my nostrils. Most of the recliners were occupied by women having poison pumped into them through tubing that slinked just beneath the middle of their collarbones like slender white tree snakes. Most were talking with their neighbors, reading, or engrossed in whatever was coming through their headphones. A few were sitting motionless, staring into space through terrified, lifeless eyes surrounded by very pale skin.

It was a real uplifting place.

I was frantic to get out of there, but I had to talk with one of the nurses to make sure that they would be comfortable poisoning me with a simple IV instead of a portacath. A slender, attractive nurse with short brown hair noticed the perplexed look on my face.

"Can I help you?" she asked.

I explained that Friday was my first chemo and I needed her to check out my veins. "Sure," she replied. Her pretty smile was a welcome reprieve from the gloom pouring out of that room. Using the index and middle fingers of her right hand, she pressed on the veins in my left forearm to assess their size, strength, and depth. Her soft touch belied the toxicity of the crap she was preparing to give me.

"Chemo nurses would die for veins like yours," she said. "They're perfect." For the first time that day I chuckled. "We'll have no problem starting an IV on you," she concluded.

At least my veins got a passing grade. She reminded me to take the antinausea drugs before I came in. I thanked her, took a quick look around, and got the hell out of there.

Although our friends and family in Fort Worth knew what was happening, word was just filtering out to my colleagues around the United States and abroad. Calls, e-mails, and letters began arriving from all over. Everyone was concerned, supportive, and wanted to help, but there wasn't much anyone could do.

One of the early callers was Dr. Barbara L, who practices in Seattle, Washington. We had taught gynecologic surgery at meetings all over the U.S. for many years and had a lot of respect for each other, both personally and professionally. Dr. Barbara had been the first female admitted to the Princeton undergraduate program after it decided that women might actually be qualified for admission. Partly because of that experience, she was endowed with a unique combination of intelligence and toughness. Nobody messed with Dr. Barbara.

After we talked for a while, she mentioned a set of audiotapes that she'd sent me. She recommended them to her patients who were beginning chemotherapy. All had found them to be inspirational and soothing during the hours while poison dripped into their veins. I thanked her for calling and promised to check them out.

When the tapes arrived the next day, I couldn't wait to find out what could be soothing and inspiring enough to make me forget what was happening. I listened to the first one even though my first dose was still two days away.

It didn't take long for me to figure out that guys don't need or want inspiration. We need beer, burgers, football, fishing, country music, television, and women; *inspiration* we can do without. On the tape, the soft, quiet, female, inspirational voice told me to envision cute little blue aliens who had just landed at the oncologist's office bringing a magic fountain filled with delightful red fluid that would eventually find its way into my vein and directly to the cancer. Once there, this alien Gatorade would punish the tumor for interfering with my life by magically melting it away! Making this discourse even worse, crappy "soothing" organ music filled the background while these little Teletubbies went about their business.

Barbara was a great friend, and I appreciated her concern, but what a pile of crap!

I decided to save the tapes for someone who needed to be inspired. I would watch the poison go in with a nice Willie Nelson tune playing in the background. I didn't need aliens and a magic fountain full of healing water to do that.

I had only one small task remaining before my chemo phase began. Missy, a Brittany and our second dog, had joined the family shortly after Jessica was born. She'd been a treasured family member for fourteen years when she died a couple of weeks after my surgery. For a dog-loving family, her loss only compounded an already stress-filled situation.

It had been weeks since my normally fun-filled, ebullient family had smiled, and that needed correcting. I was certain the cure for our collective blues was a cute, enthusiastic, cuddly puppy. After Missy died, Jenny and I had talked about finding another dog, but she wanted to wait until I finished chemo; she'd have her hands full for the next few months taking care of me. Knowing her opinion on the subject, I did what any husband recently diagnosed with cancer should: I proceeded without asking and without permission.

It took a while, but I finally found an eight-week-old chocolate lab, the only remaining female in a litter of six. The breeder was only forty-five minutes from our house, and the pup could be picked up on the same day I was scheduled to begin chemo.

Perfect.

My plan took shape. While Jenny and I were at the "infusion center," I would send Julie and Jessica to look at the puppy; they would have a signed check just in case they decided to bring her home. I figured their chances of playing with the puppy and not returning with her were approximately zero.

Boy, Jenny was really going to be pissed!

CHAPTER EIGHTEEN

July 24, 1998: Chemotherapy

The Texas summer was in full swing; it was 98 degrees on the Friday I was due to start my chemo. As I looked out the window I thought, *what a great day to get poisoned!* I'd been back at work for ten days, and my appointment with Cytoxan was for 1:00 p.m. that Friday afternoon. I'd decided to see patients in the morning to keep my mind off what lay ahead.

Since returning to my practice, I had been pleasantly surprised by the number of patients who asked about what had happened and how was I doing. Some of these ladies had been my patients for decades, during which time I had delivered their kids, done their surgeries, and listened to their troubles. My job had always been to help them with their medical problems, but now they were encouraging me. Their concern was unexpected, yet heartwarming and very humbling.

Before I left for work I gave Julie and Jessica a signed check and carefully written directions to the dog breeder's house. My daughters were more excited than I'd seen them in years. I was astounded they'd been able to keep the secret from Jenny, which was not an easy task, especially for a teenager such as Jessica.

Physically I was ready for the chemotherapy. The right side of my chest was still numb, but I'd regained most of my range of motion in my arm and shoulder. There was some pain, but it was tolerable and I could function. I wasn't up to playing golf yet, but I was hoping that would come soon.

I saw patients in the office until twelve-thirty, then drove across town and met Jenny at the Infusion Room. We were right on time, but I got the "patient treatment" immediately. The receptionist, a large, wiry-haired, angry woman with inch-thick makeup that didn't quite cover a brown mole on her nose, shoved a stack of forms and a half-chewed ballpoint pen at me.

"Here, fill these out," she commanded without the slightest bit of compassion. I figured she could take a grizzly bear without much effort, so I sheepishly took the papers, sat down, and answered the same hundred questions I'd answered a dozen times, including the previous Monday in this very same office. About halfway through the paperwork, I began wondering why patients put up with all this repetitive crap, but then I answered my own question—they put up with it because it's the only way they can see their doctor—and continued to write.

When I was finished, I handed the completed forms to "Mamuk, The Killer Receptionist" and took a chair next to Jenny. Although no one else could tell, I knew Jenny was silently laughing her ass off that I had been forced to deal with "Mamuk" just like every other patient.

Jenny really didn't need to stay around while I got infused, but I had to keep her away from the house while Julie and Jessica did the "dog deed." So that morning I had told her I thought it would be wonderful if she'd stay with me. It was a lame request and didn't sound like me at all, but she agreed.

After what seemed like an eight-hour wait, the attractive young nurse who'd checked out my veins the previous Monday stepped into the waiting room, looking for me. Wow; if chemo was a necessity, at least I was going to be poisoned by an easy-on-the-eyes nurse. For a brief moment, daydreams took my mind off what was about to happen, but those sultry visions didn't last long. The easy-on-the-eyes nurse handed my chart to Nurse Hilda, who looked as if she could be Receptionist Mamuk's twin sister, and said, "Hilda will get your IV started and should have your Adriamycin going in shortly."

It was a little disappointing, but after waiting so long, I didn't care if Dracula himself started the IV. I just wanted someone who was good at administering it. Nurse Hilda and I walked through the ominous shadows cast by the IV poles to my very own pole, which sat by my assigned recliner.

The chair to my right was occupied by a frail woman in her forties whose lips were wrinkled and cracked from dehydration. She was completely bald, and pale skin clung to her cheekbones. Despite her obvious dire circumstances, she smiled broadly as I took my seat. After I got comfortable I noticed a white, curly-haired dog resting in her lap, happy as could be.

Gently stroking her companion, the woman said, "Hi, I'm Mary. What are you here for?"

"I've got breast cancer," I said, surprising myself with how easily the words came out.

"No shit! How the hell did that happen?" I felt an immediate bond with her.

Before I could answer, the nurse came over and pulled the needle out of Mary's portacath.

"I've got pancreatic cancer," she said. "I've been doing this crap for six months." She rose from her chair. "They finally let Spot come in with me."

Spot, a solid white miniature poodle, looked up at me with his tongue hanging out in an obvious dog-grin. "See you next week." She put Spot into her tote bag. "Got to go—my husband's waiting outside in the RV."

"She's got metastatic tumors everywhere," my nurse commented after Mary had walked out of the room. "It's really sad. She probably won't last much longer. She's been getting chemo every day for six weeks and really wanted Spot to be with her, so we thought, 'What the hell, why not?' She's a character and nobody minds the dog. Anyway, let's get you going. I need your left arm."

I never saw Mary again.

In light of Mary's situation, mine didn't seem so bad, but the memory of those ulcerative craters was still vivid, and I began to question my decision. Before I could open my mouth, the IV was in and saline was coursing into a large vein in my left arm, just above my wrist. They had me; I couldn't escape.

Nurse Hilda, as it turned out, was not the evil twin of the receptionist but her alter ego. She was competent, pleasant, and personable. If I needed a "poisoner," I was glad it was Hilda.

Decadron went in first. It's a potent steroid used to minimize nausea, counteract inflammation (poison inflames everything), and increase appetite (chemotherapy can really reduce appetite.) I was very familiar with this drug and wasn't the least bit concerned when it flowed into my circulation. I could almost see it pouring into my right atrium, like water over Niagara Falls.

Next, Hilda put on a second pair of sterile gloves and picked up a syringe containing fifty cubic centimeters of an evil-looking red fluid. Immediately I knew it was the Adriamycin. Why the hell did they make it red? It should be light green, sky blue, soft violet, comforting pink, or clear. Anything other than hellfire red would be preferable. That color just screamed, "I'm going to burn the crap out of your insides!" By wearing double gloves, Hilda emphasized that point. She didn't want any of that crap touching her skin.

Without a word, she attached the syringe to my IV and began slowly pushing the red venom into me. I was transfixed as the bright fluid ran down the tubing attached to the syringe, worked its way down the IV, then disappeared beneath my skin and into my vein. I have given IV medicines thousands of times, but I'd never thought about being on the receiving end. In truth, it was terrifying.

For the past few days I'd researched Adriamycin, and I was thoroughly familiar with it. I knew its mechanism of action, its toxicity, its dosing regimen, and how it should be administered. What I *didn't* know was what it felt like to have it circulating through my body. Not knowing what to expect was maddening. Would it burn or make my muscles cramp? Would I immediately get nauseated? My heart was racing—had the Adriamycin caused that? Would I get dizzy or light-headed? My ears began ringing, and I wondered if the medicine was doing that. Then I felt warm all over and wondered if it was burning me from the inside out.

I was losing it.

With some effort, I calmed myself and tried to concentrate on symptoms that were real, not imagined. Only then did I notice that my nasal passages and sinuses were burning. It felt like someone had stuck a hot poker in both of my nostrils, but that made absolutely no sense. How in the hell could Adriamycin be affecting my sinuses? There was nothing about "sinus toxicity" in the literature. Slowly, I regained control and tried to think rationally. What was happening to me?

As suddenly as it had happened, I realized what was going on, and it was embarrassing. I was so nervous, worked up, and sure I would feel *something* that I had been hyperventilating, breathing at least sixty times a minute, four times faster than normal. My jaw was clenched shut and my lips pursed. As a result, I was forcing air in and out of my nose as fast as I could, completely drying out my nostrils and sinuses. In the process of panicking, I'd created my own personal version of an eye-watering, nose-drying West Texas dust storm blowing through my sinuses right there in the Infusion Room.

I opened my mouth, forced myself to slow my breathing, and desperately tried to regain control. Sure enough, in a few moments I was fine.

Twenty years in medicine coupled with fear of the unknown had effortlessly overwhelmed any advantage my profession should have provided. Once again, I had reverted back to my patient mode.

I decided that I'd experienced enough of that mode; I was a doctor and I would handle my treatment like a physician. No more overactive imagination, made-up symptoms, or hyperventilating. No more patient responses. When my breathing returned to normal and my sinuses cleared, I thanked Nurse Hilda for her skill and patience, put a Willie Nelson CD in my player, plugged in the headphones, and waited for the Cytoxan. I didn't give a damn what they named the stuff, I just wanted it so I could get out of there.

Not surprisingly, I felt absolutely nothing during the hour or so it took my new best friend, Cytoxan, to join my innards. No symptoms, no side effects, no problems, nothing. Willie and I did just fine, no aliens needed, thank you.

Three hours after it all began, my IV was out and I rose from the recliner, a little wobbly but pleased to have Round One completed. I felt great. Obviously the nausea, fatigue, and body aches supposedly associated with chemo weren't real but were mostly the result of patients' uncontrolled fears and anxiety. Since I was a doctor and had both recognized and controlled what had happened earlier, my arrogance led me to believe I could handle the chemo just fine. No nausea medicines were necessary, just a little knowledge. I left the Infusion Room pretty impressed with myself.

Jenny had made friends with everyone in the waiting room by the time I reappeared. "How was it?" she asked.

"Piece of cake, no problem. Let's get out of here."

"What would you like for dinner?" she asked as we headed home. "Name it, I'll fix it."

That was easy. My favorite meal consisted of a thick rib eye, medium-rare; a baked potato; grilled asparagus; and a good bottle of wine.

Jenny dropped me off at home (not noticing that Julie's car was gone) and took off for the grocery store. I walked into the house with a broad smile on my face. Chemo number one was over and it had been easy, nothing to it. A small glass of wine couldn't hurt. A great dinner was in the works, and a new puppy should arrive any minute. This cancer thing might not be so bad after all.

A short while later, while I was pouring the wine and Jenny was working on the asparagus, a loud, distinctive noise came from downstairs. Julie had roared up the driveway and into her parking spot, stopping just short of the front wall.

I hid my grin and figured the fun was about to begin, and that soon I'd find out how badly I'd screwed up in Jenny's eyes.

"Where have the girls been?" my wife asked, mildly perturbed.

"Beats me," I lied, punctuating it with a gulp of wine.

Julie was first up the stairs, grinning from ear to ear.

"Just where have you and your sister been?" Jenny asked, giving Julie her best "mother" look, which only intensified when Jessica came into the kitchen carrying a little, fuzzy, flop-eared chocolate-brown thing with a red bandana tied around its neck. The ball of fur was curled into a knot in her arms, half asleep.

The girls laughed, looked at their mother, and blurted out, "Well, what do you think?"

Jenny's "mother look" shifted to me as she took the puppy from Jessica. Even from where I was, I could see that the puppy was scared and shaking a bit. Suddenly it let out a squeaky bark and licked Jenny square on her nose, its tail whooshing with delight.

"Daaaaammmmmn!" Jenny drew out the word for at least fifteen seconds, then gave me another pissed look. She held that squirming bundle of fun at arm's length, looked her square in those big brown eyes, kissed her on the nose, and said, "Welcome home, sweetheart."

The stress of the previous few weeks melted away as Jenny sat on the kitchen floor playing with the newest Johns family member and began to cry.

Since Julie and Jessica had been willing participants in my scheme, Jenny gave them the honor of cooking dinner while she held, cuddled, and welcomed "No Name" to her brood. She knew exactly the responsibility this little creature represented; the kids just knew the puppy was cute and fun. But joy and happiness filled every inch of our kitchen for the first time in a while.

The puppy rested in Jenny's lap as we enjoyed a wonderful family dinner. I gorged myself on the best rib eye and red wine I'd ever tasted, still wondering what all the fuss over chemotherapy was about. I guessed that most folks just didn't know what I'd figured out. I felt a little queasy, but fine. The girls and I cleaned up the kitchen (Jenny still had the puppy in her arms), and then we introduced the puppy to her crate.

I went to bed early. For some reason I was more tired than usual; my stressful day probably accounted for that. Tomorrow would be fun with the new addition around.

A few hours later, however, the proverbial shit hit the fan. About midnight, No Name had been howling in her crate for about an hour, and I'd begun to notice a bit of epigastric discomfort. That was strange, because steak and wine had always been my comfort food. I desperately tried to get back to sleep, but I did nothing but toss and turn for the next thirty minutes. Then came a sensation that felt like an eight-pound, red-hot bowling ball had slammed into my stomach. It was my first clue that steak, wine, Adriamycin, and Cytoxan might not be particularly compatible.

Waves of nausea soon accompanied the pain and were quickly joined by a cacophony of horrendous abdominal cramps. There was no doubt about what was coming next, and it wouldn't be pretty. I introduced my face to the toilet, an acquaintance that continued for the next six hours. Jenny stuffed Compazine (an anti-nausea drug) in a couple of orifices, but it didn't help. I spent the most miserable night of my life with both arms wrapped around the toilet bowl.

Mercifully, by morning the vomiting had lessened a bit, but I felt like someone had given me a large intravenous dose of Ebola virus. Jenny had been up with me all night and was in a sorry mood. "Did you take the nausea medicine before you went in?" she asked, suspecting she already knew the answer.

"No," I sheepishly replied. "I'm a doctor, damn it. I didn't figure I needed it."

"You are a dumb shit!" She gave me her "mother look," full-throttle. "I bet you'll listen to them next time, *Doctor.*" With that, she finally drifted off to sleep.

She was absolutely right. Because of my own arrogance, I was suffering with unrelenting seasickness, without the fun of being on a boat. All I could do was take drugs and cling to what Dr. N and the infusion nurse had said: "If you get nauseated, it shouldn't last for more than twenty-four to thirty-six hours."

I really looked forward to Sunday morning. It had to be better than this.

Sunday morning finally came, and I found out the damn doctor had lied again. "Twenty-four to thirty-six hours," my ass! I felt worse. The seasickness was unrelenting, and my stomach burned like fire. Medicine didn't help, and nothing I ate made any difference. I had discovered what true suffering was. No matter what remedy I tried, a fresh wave of nausea hit every thirty minutes. For a fleeting moment I thought about marijuana. Grass was pretty popular when I was in college, but I had never tried it.

In medical school we had been reminded constantly that if we got a felony conviction, we would no longer be eligible for a professional license and couldn't practice medicine. Drug possession was a felony in Texas. By 1998, however, it was well documented that marijuana was great at counteracting many of the more common side effects of chemotherapy, particularly nausea. I was miserable enough to consider trying it, but knew I couldn't. The risk was simply too great.

Since marijuana wasn't really an option for me, I gave in and took the "heavy hitter" Kytril, the most potent antinausea drug available. At fifty bucks a tablet, it should have been able to make a pizza sound good again. Four tablets and two hundred dollars later, my love affair with the toilet bowl was abating a little.

By Sunday evening the nausea finally began to improve. Unfortunately it was replaced by a constant burning sensation in my upper abdomen, as if the hot bowling ball was still there but had shrunk a bit. Both oncologists had said these symptoms would be gone in two or three days, so I figured Monday would be no problem. I popped a couple of Compazine tablets, thanked everyone for helping, kissed the new puppy, and went to bed, anticipating a better day.

Of course I was wrong. I awakened Monday morning feeling just as bad as I'd felt Sunday. I wanted to dope myself up and stay in bed, but I needed to make a living. Against Jenny's advice, I stuffed my pockets full of Compazine, Kytril, and saltine crackers, crawled into my car, and headed to the office.

By two that afternoon, I'd spent more time in the bathroom than with patients. By day's end, my nurses claimed I looked worse than a newly pregnant woman with hyperemesis (severe morning sickness).

"Thanks, a lot," I told them, then headed out the back door. Tomorrow would be better, I was sure of it, but home sounded pretty good right then.

While I was becoming more and more intimately acquainted with the porcelain throne, our fluffy brown pup remained the bright spot of my otherwise miserable existence. She was beginning to acclimate to her new home and had already made friends with Ernie, the grumpy old stray cat that had joined our family a few years earlier.

The puppy was having a great time chewing everything that fit in her mouth and discovering new and exciting places to urinate. Julie and Jessica were on the floor laughing and playing with her when I came home from work.

"How did it go?" Jenny asked.

"Not worth a crap." I headed to my recliner.

The kids brought the puppy over and put her in my lap. That little chocolate ball of fur put her front paws on my chest and tried to lick the whiskers off my face, her long brown tail whishing back and forth like a windshield wiper.

Suddenly I didn't need Kytril or Compazine; she was better medicine than any pill I had swallowed (or put anywhere else) for the past three days. It was amazing how much difference a little puppy could make.

"You think the patients would mind if she came to the office with me for a few days?" I asked.

"Forget it!" they replied in unison. "You go, but she stays. You're not having all the fun."

"She needs a name!" Jessica yelled over the ruckus.

"How about Chemo?" I asked sarcastically, knowing my family would unanimously reject that one.

"Her name has got to mean something to *you*," Jessica said. "You're responsible for bringing her here, and she sure seems to make you feel better."

My daughter was right. I studied the dog for a moment and thought about the things that brought me happiness. Of course my wife and daughters were first on the list, but I couldn't imagine naming the dog after one of them. Then, suddenly, I thought about my Harley-Davidson motorcycle. I'd acquired it under unusual circumstances, too.

In 1984, two colleagues and I had established the first in vitro fertilization (IVF) center in Fort Worth. Partnering with UT Southwestern Medical Center and Harris Methodist Hospital, we founded and developed the program, and our first "test-tube" baby was born in 1986.

About a year before my breast cancer diagnosis, I had finished the infertility evaluation of a young couple who lived in a small town sixty miles south of Fort Worth. Linda and Mike were in their late twenties and managed an apartment complex in their hometown. They were good, hardworking folks and wanted a baby badly. After Linda's evaluation, it was obvious that their only option for pregnancy was IVF. Unfortunately, the technology was very expensive (and remains so now).

When they came back to the office a few days later, I explained the IVF process to them, but to no avail. Linda said they couldn't possibly afford it. I nodded and was about to leave the exam room when Mike spoke up:

"I've got a 1973 Harley-Davidson that I've been working on. I'll sell it and we'll use the money to do that test-tube thing."

Linda gave him a relieved and grateful smile.

"Sounds good to me," I said, opening the door. "See you in a couple of months." But I never made it out of the room. I stopped, turned around, and shut the door.

"I'll make you a deal," I said as they stood, ready to leave. A little startled, they sat back down. "You give me the Harley and I'll get you pregnant, Linda." Immediately I realized how inappropriate that sounded. "What I mean is, I'll do as many IVF cycles as it takes for you to get pregnant. Then I get the Harley."

"Deal!" Mike said, wasting no time. He shook my hand as his wife collapsed into tears.

"You don't know how much we appreciate this," Linda said.

I'd wanted a motorcycle for as long as I could remember, but Jenny and the kids had absolutely forbidden me from buying one. They were convinced it was too dangerous. I'd given up on the idea long ago, until Mike mentioned his Harley.

This was my chance, and I jumped on it. Surely my family wouldn't stand in the way of this lovely couple having the child they so desperately wanted!

For the rest of the day I grinned like a Cheshire cat. I couldn't wait to get home and tell Jenny and the kids. They weren't happy, but they agreed to the deal as long as I met their terms and rules. I gleefully agreed and plowed ahead with Linda's IVF cycle the very next week.

With great pride I called Linda a few weeks later. Her pregnancy test was positive! Helping a couple with infertility had always been one of the happiest, most rewarding parts of my job, and these two kids were ecstatic. Their joy multiplied when, four weeks later, an ultrasound confirmed that she was carrying triplets! I had never been hugged so much as when the couple saw those babies on the ultrasound screen. Linda had a remarkably uneventful pregnancy and delivery, and I got my much-coveted Harley.

A few weeks after the triplets were born, their local newspaper ran a front-page story with the headline "Local Couple Trade Motorcycle for Triplets," complete with a picture of Mom and Dad holding their three babies. Unfortunately, the story also included my name and office address.

Almost immediately, my nurses were inundated with phone calls offering a chicken for a pap smear, an old hunting dog for a mammogram, an aluminum boat with a ten-horsepower motor for a hysterectomy, and a twelve-gage pump shotgun for a complete physical. The offers kept coming for weeks. Before my practice became a gynecologic pawn shop, I ended my days of bartering as quickly as they had begun.

I had the Harley restored to showroom condition, with one small exception. I had an electric starter installed, hidden beneath the black leather seat. I loved to kick-start the bike, imagining myself as Peter Fonda in *Easy Rider*. However, the older Harleys tended to backfire as one jumped down on the kick-start pedal, and a broken leg was often the result, so I added the electric starter. When no one was around, I just hit the starter button and roared off. When I had an audience, particularly if it included women, I would put on my helmet, zip up my black leather jacket, cock my head to one side, grin, and kick-start that baby. My Harley became legendary in the three-block radius around my house (the only place my family allowed me to ride).

Considering my love for the cherry-red, antique motorcycle and the way I got it, I looked at our new pup and figured Harley was the perfect name for her.

"Harley. I want to name her Harley-Davidson Dog," I said to my family.

After a spirited discussion, we finally agreed on Harley. The pup let out an excited bark and immediately peed on the carpet. We figured she liked it, too. It didn't take long until Harley (the dog) completely and forever displaced Harley (the motorcycle) in my heart. She's still there.

CHAPTER NINETEEN

Chemo

After suffering with nausea for a week, I finally began to feel semihuman again. Although I didn't have an appetite and felt the constant undercurrent of a sick stomach, it wasn't as horrific as it had been earlier. I was beginning to understand how my obstetric patients felt when they suffered from nausea early in pregnancy. Since I'd never been pregnant, I had assumed that pregnancy nausea really couldn't be as bad as they claimed. My remedy for my patients had always been the same: crackers and peanut butter. At the time, there was no safe antinausea drug for pregnant women, and although I thought the peanut-butter-and-cracker treatment was nonsense, the two foods were safe and nutritious and certainly would do no harm.

I was thankful my chemo-induced nausea would last only five months instead of the nine agonizing months some of my pregnant patients had to endure. I also felt fortunate that when I was finally through with my chemo, I wouldn't have to take a baby home and raise it.

One Sunday morning I was desperate and really tired of the constant, unrelenting nausea. On a whim, I decided to try the peanut-butter-and-cracker remedy. Eight hours later I had knocked back an entire box of saltines and a small jar of creamy peanut butter. Those calories weren't going to help my love handles, but shockingly the nausea was almost non-existent. As long as I ate a saltine cracker slathered with peanut butter every fifteen minutes, I could function. Wow—not only did I feel better, but also I had actually given my patients good advice. How comforting. My own arrogance was becoming annoying.

By Monday morning I had stocked the top drawer of my desk with a large stash of saltines and one jar each of smooth and crunchy peanut butter (since smooth worked, crunchy might even be better). My four-month peanut-butter-and-cracker love fest had begun, and I would highly recommend it for anyone who's pregnant or being poisoned.

My workday began at eight that morning with Maureen, a forty-seven-year-old lady who lived on a nearby ranch. Her reason for coming in was simply listed as "to talk."

I introduced myself and sat down across from her in the exam room. She was a slender woman with a pleasant face framed with short brown hair. Her green eyes looked tired. The bright yellow long-sleeve blouse she wore was tucked into her jeans, which covered her round-toed riding boots.

She squirmed and cleared her throat as her eyes grew wider and her gaze more fearful. From experience I assumed her demeanor reflected an imminent divorce or an unexpected pregnancy. I was wrong on both counts, and my professional world would take a radical turn a few months later because of her visit.

"I called Cynthia, and she told me what you're going through," Maureen said. "She said we should talk. Said you wouldn't mind."

Cynthia was my neighbor, friend, patient, and a breast cancer survivor.

"My mother died of breast cancer five years ago," Maureen continued, then blinked rapidly to hold back tears. "After my mammogram, the doctor called and said he saw something that had to be removed." Her voice cracked and she cleared her throat. "I saw a surgeon yesterday; he has me scheduled next week for a mastectomy and node dissection. I'm so scared."

Maureen was filled with the same terror I had experienced a scant four months ago. In an instant my mind raced so fast that I had no idea what to say. The exam room walls began to close in on me, and my chest tightened.

I closed my eyes for a moment. I had to collect myself quickly, but the memories of my cancer were simply too fresh.

"Excuse me a minute." I got up and walked out of the exam room. I managed to get myself down the short hall to my office. I sat down, grabbed a cracker out of my desk, spread a big wad of Skippy Chunky on top, got up, walked back into the exam room, sat down, and took a big bite.

Maureen stared at me and my peanut butter cracker, and her expression twisted into shock. "What are you doing?"

I guess she'd never seen a doctor having a snack in the exam room during a visit. "Oh, nothing, just making sure I don't throw up on you during the exam," I said, choking down the last bite.

After I explained about my nausea and the benefits of my snack, she finally smiled, and the mood lightened enough for us to continue our talk. We spent the next few minutes discussing what had happened since her mammogram. The longer we talked, the more composed and rational she became. We discussed mammograms, biopsies, lymph nodes, and surgery. Most importantly, we spoke about how she needed to get the best possible recommendations— not the quickest.

No one had discussed sentinel node technology with her, so I suggested an appointment with Dr. Marilyn L in Dallas.

"Dallas?" she asked. "Can't I see someone here?"

"You already have, and they didn't mention sentinel nodes, so I suggest another opinion before you decide what to do," I said. "I'll help you get through this, but everything has to be done right, and not necessarily tomorrow. Breast cancer is a psychological emergency, not a medical one. The more doctors who evaluate your case, the better the recommendations will be." A few minutes later Maureen left my office with her Dallas appointment confirmed.

About ten days later, Dr. L called me. "How are you doing, Alan?" Marilyn asked, sounding bright and cheery.

"I'm doing okay. What's up?"

"You sent Maureen over. We did her surgery yesterday. Very interesting. Her sentinel node was in the internal mammary chain; that's very unusual. It was also positive for tumor. Her axillary nodes were negative."

Dr. L was saying that Maureen's tumor had spread to a lymph node beneath her sternum, not to the expected place—the armpit nodes. Sentinel node technology was the only way this would have been discovered, since the nodes to which her cancer had spread are not routinely checked or removed. Had Maureen undergone a simple mastectomy and axillary node dissection, as originally recommended, no one would have known about the tumor-laden node in the center of her chest until her disease had spread, possibly to the point of being incurable.

I thanked Dr. L and hung up, my mind spinning like a gyroscope. What had happened with Maureen was, in a way, extremely sobering and frightening. Maureen had been one short conversation away from the wrong operation, one that could have ultimately resulted in metastatic cancer and death. She'd faced the same decisions I had been forced to consider, but without the inside knowledge and contacts that I had so heavily relied on. We were both lucky, but many others were not.

Maureen was just the first of hundreds of patients, men and women, who were newly diagnosed with breast cancer and who sought my advice, counsel, and reassurance in the years that followed. Neither Maureen nor I realized it at the time, but she had planted the seeds for what would become Fort Worth's first and only comprehensive breast center. But that would come much later.

Thanks to peanut butter, crackers, and the addition of Blue Bell ice cream, the next couple of weeks went well. My energy and appetite returned, and I could *almost* suppress memories of my first chemo. Although fully back into my doctor mode, I had learned a valuable patient lesson: When an oncologist says, "Take your antinausea medicines before you get the chemotherapy," it's a good idea to follow instructions. For my next round of chemotherapy, which was just around the corner, I acquired loads of antinausea drugs and I planned to use the maximum prescribed doses, maybe even an extra one or two.

Besides the nausea, I was worried about my hair. Dr. N had warned me it would fall out soon. Every morning I would give it a good yank, just to check. So far my trademark full head of hair was fine, and I was anxious to get Round Two over with.

A visit with Dr. N in his office initiated my next chemo. "How did it go the first time?" he asked.

"Fine" I said, ignoring what had actually happened.

"Bull," Jenny said. "If he'd done what you told him to do, he would have been fine, but *nooooo*, he's a *doctor*. He was sicker than hell for a week."

"You did take the meds this time, didn't you?" each of them asked at different times during our meeting.

"Oh yeah!" My speech was beginning to slur a bit from the massive dose of antinausea drugs I'd taken a few minutes earlier.

"Notice anything with your hair?" Dr. N asked.

"It's fine." I grabbed a handful and yanked just to emphasize the point.

"You will." He rubbed his bald scalp and grinned. "Your blood counts were okay, so you're ready for the next dose."

My blood counts may have been ready, but suddenly my brain wasn't. I was just starting to feel human again, and I had to repeat the torture. I knew it was necessary, but going back into the Infusion Room knowing what was going to happen in the next few days was difficult, at best.

Jenny left, saying she would pick me up when I was finished. I said okay, because I knew she didn't want to risk getting another puppy. The walk to my recliner in the "cancer gas station" was completely different this time. There was no terror, no mystery, and no sweaty palms, just acquiescence. Maybe Round One had given me a better perspective, or (more likely) the large dose of anti-nausea drugs I had on board relaxed me, but the apprehension that had been so prominent three weeks before was gone. I didn't even notice the ominous shadows from the IV poles that had been so foreboding the last time.

I got comfortable in my recliner and offered my left arm to the infusion nurse. Once again, I was the only male there. "How's Mary?" I asked my nurse.

My question was answered by a blank, sad stare and stone-cold silence from the others. With that cheery start, I began infusion cycle number two. The gloom and sadness in the room was palpable. The nurses loved what they did and took the loss of a patient very personally. To make the situation even worse, the room was filled with patients who had befriended Mary and shared her daily struggle. They'd even grown fond of Spot. It was becoming obvious what each person in the Infusion Room represented to the other patients: Hope with a capital "H." If any one of us lost our fight, everyone's deepest, most repressed fears blossomed and surfaced with a vengeance.

Amid the gloom, the Adriamycin (or Red Devil, as I began calling it) went in without a hitch. Meanwhile, two ladies positioned themselves in their recliners on either side of me. Each was there for her first "poisoning session." The gray-haired lady on my right, who looked to be about sixty, wore a floral tent dress. I didn't get her name, so I called her "Right."

On my left sat an obviously frightened, slender lady in her forties with short blonde hair and beautiful blue eyes. I called her "Left." Her yellow and white blouse and dark green pants matched her lime-colored spike heels. She was dressed as if she'd just finished a shopping trip at Neiman Marcus.

Simultaneously, both asked what I had and why I was getting chemo. My answer brought the now familiar "No Shit!" from Right and a more restrained, polite "Oh, my goodness!" from Left. Both ladies had been diagnosed with breast cancer and had no idea it could happen in men.

"How did your first chemo go?" Right asked.

"Fine, no problem," I lied. "You both took the nausea meds before you came, didn't you?"

"Of course; my doctor told me to," Left said, followed quickly by "Me, too. Why wouldn't I?" from Right. Both had the same oncologist and obviously listened to him, unlike the centerpiece of this trio. A little embarrassed, I asked no more questions.

"You'll do fine. Just stay away from red wine and steak tonight. It doesn't sit well with this stuff." I pointed toward my IV, which had just emptied. "Stay on the drugs, like your doctor says. It'll keep you from getting nauseated."

After my IV was removed, I wished them well and started to walk out, but not before offering one last pearl of wisdom.

"If you get nauseated, try peanut butter and saltine crackers. It works like a charm."

"You sound like my old obstetrician!" Right said.

"He sounds like a smart doctor!" I replied, and strolled out with an impish grin.

I left the cancer gas station knowing that a rough few days lay ahead, but I was thankful my hair was still intact. Maybe I would be the exception and keep it. I wasn't excited about being bald.

A nice bowl of chicken soup awaited me at home. No wine or steak. I'd learned my lesson on that one. Since peanut butter had worked, Jenny decided I should try another old, reliable, grandmother remedy, so homemade chicken soup was on the menu.

Shortly after midnight, I learned another rule of the chemo world. After being poisoned, never, ever eat anything that you really don't want to see again in a few hours. The soup looked pretty much the same coming out as it did going in. I haven't been able to tolerate chicken soup since that night.

The pre-chemo medicines helped for a few hours, but about midnight the same old crap hit again, not as intense, but every bit as relentless. After trying oral drugs for a while, I was reduced again to the ultimate humiliation—suppositories. I finally fell sleep for a few hours.

By morning the "chemo flu" started again. This time, however, I was prepared. I wasn't working for a couple of days so I could take my drugs and be miserable at home. I was happy about this, because throwing up in front of a patient never filled her with confidence. Besides, home was where the heart and the new puppy resided.

A week later, the chemo effects were better, thanks to peanut butter and tincture of time. While showering after my morning run, I thought about how quickly the family had adapted to my every-three-week regimen: one week of hell followed by a two-week case of slowly-improving Ebola, then start the whole damn thing all over again.

As I stepped out of the shower, something strange caught my eye. The shower floor looked muddy. I hadn't run through any puddles, but the bottom of the shower looked as if I'd rinsed off a pound of dirt.

Then I glanced at my fluffy white towel. It was covered with a barely visible layer of brown hair, the same color as mine. Glancing in the mirror, I saw that both shoulders were covered with light brown hair, also just like mine. Just to confirm my suspicions, I grabbed a handful of hair and gave it a yank. The entire wad came out without any pain. I picked up my comb and ran it through my hair. Every tooth of it was clogged with hair. The amount of hair in the shower, on the towel, and in the sink was astounding. Before I combed myself bald, I decided to try hair spray, thinking it might glue down what little hair remained on my head.

Although my hair had always been plentiful (*full*, my barber called it), at the current rate of loss I had enough to last only a day or two. Baldness was obviously coming soon, and it seemed like a once-in-a-lifetime opportunity for some fun. If I was going to be bald, I might as well enjoy it.

The office was pretty uneventful that morning. I was talking with one of my longtime patients after we'd finished her annual checkup. She had been my patient for nineteen years, and I had delivered all three of her kids.

We talked about her children, her job, and her husband before turning to her only medical complaint—her hair was falling out. Every day her brush was full of hair, and she was afraid she would become bald.

Thinning hair is very common among women in their forties and fifties, but contrary to what they are told, the problem isn't hormone-related (men tend to blame everything on their wives' hormones). Women losing hair at that time in their lives is an entirely natural process and almost always self-limited, reversing itself in a few months with no treatment at all.

Rather than give her the medical explanation, though, I just smiled and said, "You think you've got a problem? Look at this!" With that, I grabbed a big handful of my hair, yanked it out, then said, "Now *that* is falling-out hair!"

Her eyes bugged out, her mouth fell open, and she nearly fell off the exam table before I could explain what was going on. After she caught her breath, we both had a good laugh. She hasn't asked about her hair since.

After pulling the same trick a few more times, my head had become a patchwork of pale skin interrupted by tufts of hair—I looked like someone with a terminal fungal disease of the scalp.

Back home, Harley was adjusting quickly to all of her new surroundings, with the exception of her crate. She hated the crate. After we put her in for the night, she wailed for hours as if we were beating her with a shoe. Finally she'd fall asleep from sheer exhaustion. She didn't sleep much, and we slept even less.

One night after my second round of chemo, Jenny and the kids had gone to visit Jenny's dad in Greenville, so it was just me and the howler left at home. After dinner and some playing, I crated her and went to bed. Her incessant wailing started immediately.

After a full hour of her woo-woo-wooooing, I could take no more. I went downstairs and, of course, she gleefully stopped crying the instant I opened the crate door and took her out. Cuddled in my arms, she licked me on the nose and immediately went to sleep.

Damn, I'm going to get myself in trouble with Jenny for this one, but this dog is not going back into the crate.

I carried her upstairs, where I gently laid her on the foot of our bed, turned out the light, and crawled in. About thirty seconds later, she crawled up to my pillow, curled herself around the top of my almost bald head, rested her muzzle on my cheek, let out a contented sigh, and fell sound asleep. Not a single peep came out of her the rest of the night. Twelve years later, she still curls herself around my head, rests her muzzle on my neck, and sleeps in the same spot. She's seventy pounds now and takes up most of my pillow, but I don't mind at all.

CHAPTER TWENTY

Joan

I wasn't dealing well with chemo, nausea, hair loss, fear, and all the other issues that went along with my disease. So I was thankful when I received a much-needed phone call from a patient named Joan, whom I'd operated on four months before I'd discovered my inverted nipple. Word of my cancer diagnosis had spread through the community. "Alan, can we talk?" Her request sounded more like a command and reminded me how much I respected this strong, determined woman when I first met her in my office eight months earlier.

Joan, a very attractive lady in her forties, was my first patient on a blustery December day in 1997. She sat poised in the exam room, dressed in a lavender silk blouse and skirt that offset her slender figure and blond hair. A white pearl necklace circled her neck. Despite the fact that she was in a doctor's office to discuss surgery, she exuded confidence and intelligence.

Her cheerful personality and bright smile were a welcome start to my day. I suggested we begin with her medical history, and she quickly summed up what had happened to her during the past fourteen years. Since beginning my practice, I had heard thousands of medical histories, some unimaginably tragic but most pretty routine. However, Joan's history was truly sobering, inspiring, and medically fascinating.

Joan explained that she'd been diagnosed with breast cancer in 1983, only three months after her thirtieth birthday. Following a mastectomy, she endured what was by today's standards relentless, almost barbaric chemotherapy. She not only recovered but also thrived, continuing to manage her business and even finding time for volunteer work. A few years after she'd been declared disease free, she and her husband adopted a daughter.

In 1992, ten years after her first diagnosis and three months before her fortieth birthday, Joan discovered a lump in her remaining breast. A few days later her suspicions were confirmed: The demon had returned and she had breast cancer again.

Her newly diagnosed cancer, separate from and unrelated to the first, was treated with a mastectomy followed by chemotherapy and radiation. After bilateral mastectomies and two full courses of chemotherapy, it was obvious that her will and determination were formidable. Because our first meeting had been four months before my diagnosis, I didn't truly understand the psychological ramifications having cancer. I simply was amazed at the way she'd been able to convert her fear into a fighting spirit.

And fight she did.

A few short months after her second cycle of surgery, chemotherapy, and weeks of radiation, she was back to volunteering at a camp for grieving children. Then, five months after Joan's second diagnosis, her mother was diagnosed with breast cancer, further complicating her life. Within a year, she and Rozanne, her college roommate and lifelong friend, co-chaired Fort Worth's first Race for the Cure. By then, hundreds of women who had been newly diagnosed with breast cancer had sought Joan's advice and counsel, which she willingly gave. She began to make it her life's mission to help as many women as possible navigate the shark-infested waters that constitute breast cancer.

A scant four years later, in late 1997, Joan discovered a lump in her armpit, which became her third bout with breast cancer. Somehow, despite everything, a small outgrowth of cancer had remained in her armpit and took four years to show itself. Another surgery and weeks of radiation therapy followed. I did not know it at the time, but her case was just one of dozens I would see that emphasized, in my opinion, the need for a truly comprehensive breast center in Fort Worth in order to standardize and optimize the medical, surgical, and psychological care of breast cancer patients.

After her last diagnosis, she was referred to me for a laparoscopic hysterectomy in an effort to prevent another recurrence. Not only had she faced breast cancer three times in fourteen years, but also her hysterectomy would force her to cope with early menopause and hot flashes.

Her surgery was scheduled for a few weeks later, and the procedure went fine. To no one's surprise, Joan proved to be one tough, impressive patient. At 7:00 a.m. the morning after I'd done her surgery, I knocked on her hospital room door very softly, not wanting to startle her awake. Hearing a prompt "Come in," I opened the door only to find Joan standing beside her hospital bed, dressed (complete with heels), her makeup immaculate, her hair brushed and perfect, asking why I was so late for my post-op rounds! She had things to do and people to help; there was no time for hospitals.

I laughed, got out of her way, and she was gone before I made it back to the nurses' station. A couple of weeks later, she had recovered and was back to her frenetic pace.

Six months later, when she called and asked if we could talk, I quickly agreed. I was barely into the first hundred yards of my race with breast cancer, and I knew I could learn a lot from Joan. This conversation with her was the start of a role reversal, the first of many I would experience during the coming months, in which a patient counseled her doctor. Little did we know that ten years later, our experiences with breast cancer would culminate with something that at that time was unimaginable for both of us. During the call, Joan and I made plans to meet at my house.

"Wow! You're really going to listen to somebody?" Jenny quipped after I hung up. "Maybe this cancer thing is going to be good for you after all!" Although we didn't realize it, Jenny's comment was prophetic.

A few days later, the doorbell rang. Harley ran, barking, to the front door, slipping and sliding on the hardwood floor and wagging her entire hindquarters as only a puppy could. Joan walked in, and Harley attacked her left shoe. She laughed and gave Harley her shoe as we sat down at the kitchen table.

Immediately Joan pulled a small ceramic elephant and a rather elaborately decorated eighteen-inch wand out of her purse.

Jenny and I stared at the elephant and the wand for a few moments. We were trying to be polite, but we had no clue what they were for or what Joan had in mind. Joan must have both anticipated and sensed our confusion and quickly explained that during the past fourteen years, she had developed the perfect formula for battling cancer. She approached cancer treatment the same way she would approach eating an elephant: one bite at a time.

She held up my new ceramic elephant and explained that it was a metaphor to remind me that, although cancer is an all-consuming, overwhelmingly complex problem that encompasses an endless series of challenges, I had to tackle it one bite at a time. Rather than worry about surgery, chemotherapy, radiation, reconstruction, and rehabilitation all at once, I should take what was immediately in front of me, grab that bite, chew it well, swallow, then go on to the next. Before I knew it, the elephant would be gone.

Joan had been through more than most anyone I knew, and I respected her a lot, so I continued to listen. She explained that I had been trying to tackle my cancer all at once by worrying about treatment that hadn't happened yet, complications that might not occur, and problems that lay far in the future. Instead, she said, I should be focused on today. Just get through today. Worry about tomorrow when it comes.

She was right. My mind had been consumed with planning for every eventuality, and I was wearing out.

"Take one bite and chew it," Joan said. "Don't even think about the next bite."

Then she picked up the wand. Although it was pretty cool looking, it wasn't miraculous and had no supernatural powers. It simply represented all the people who were there to help me: my family, friends, doctors, and nurses.

I nodded. A lot of people were in my corner. I had an extremely loyal family, friends who were willing to drop everything to be there, and well-trained professionals directing my care.

She held the wand higher, drew it through the air, then laughed. "It's silly, I know, but it worked for me and it will work for you. When the fight seems endless and hopeless, grab the wand. It will remind you none of us are alone."

She handed me the wand and I took it, hoping to feel just a little magic. But something better happened. The moment I grasped my new "magic" wand, I felt powerful and in control, as if it really were endowed with magical powers. Like Harry Potter might do, I waved it in the air and chanted, "Out, nausea. Out of me, I say." I still felt a little queasy, but the sheer silliness of the scene made me feel better.

I took a closer look at my magic wand. Brass wire encircled a gold and black handle that merged into a fishlike figurine on one end; a circular, pink-and-gray polished stone adorned the other. With a little imagination, I could see Harry Potter using it to conjure up some sorcery or combat evil. I had an almost overwhelming urge to point my new "weapon" at something and zap it. Therein lay its power; it gave me the idea I *had* power. Of course I knew the brass-and-stone wand was not endowed with any supernatural qualities, but when I held it in my hand, it produced a childlike rush of hope and a hefty dose of endorphins.

Joan continued to explain that when things were overwhelming and out of control, she grabbed her wand and waved it around at the current "enemy," which might be nausea, chemotherapy, surgery, fatigue, hopelessness, pain, or any of the thousand hellions that constitute cancer treatment. For those few seconds, she was back in control, summoning an inner force to fight the cancer demons. And when reality returned, when the fight seemed endless and hopeless, the wand represented our *real* support, our "magic"— family, friends, doctors, and nurses.

I found Joan's approach to dealing with cancer to be disarmingly simple but very profound. I smiled. Her method of coping with the disease was starting to make a lot of sense. Although I'm not much into magic fountains and little blue aliens, her coping mechanisms struck a chord in me that was doable and helpful, and I needed that.

I knew about the physical demands of breast cancer, but I had a lot to learn about the psychological ones. I had been so busy practicing the *science* of medicine that I had inadvertently minimized the *art* of medicine. As soon as I was given my diagnosis, my "team" started planning my treatment. Until my conversation with Joan, I hadn't realized that I didn't possess the skills to cope with the overwhelming feelings that a cancer diagnosis brings. I was trained to diagnose and "cut out" problems, not to treat the emotional devastation that a cancer diagnosis brings. Joan had given me the simple tools with which I could fight the psychological battle that lay ahead.

During that visit, Joan taught me more about what patients *really* need than I had learned during my twenty years of practicing medicine. Sure, I knew what they needed medically and surgically, but my patients also needed methods to help them survive all the psychological *stuff*, too. Treating both the disease *and* the patient makes cancer treatment infinitely more survivable. Patients need to feel in control of their body and life no matter what their diagnosis is. They also need to be reminded that folks care about them—even their doctors.

My wand still occupies a special place in my study as a constant reminder of this.

For the next four months, Joan made a point to check on me during the week leading up to each new round of chemotherapy. She knew that was a particularly dark and foreboding time for me. On the Friday mornings when I left for my date with poison, I always found a small gift at my front door to remind me that one more bite of that damn elephant was about to be gone.

A few weeks after I spoke with Joan, I decided it was time to address my hair issue. My hair had always been a source of pride, but now I looked like a man who'd dumped a gallon of Rogaine on his head in a desperate attempt to stave off baldness. Clumps of thinning, dried-out, gray-brown hair were hanging on my scalp like weeds in a neglected garden that hadn't been watered in a month.

It was time. What was left of my hair had to go.

I had spent my career taking ovaries apart and putting them back together, so I figured I could shave my head with no problem. Another half-baked idea took shape.

I didn't want to spend the afternoon vacuuming hair off the carpet, and I wanted to be rid of the rest of my hair quickly, so I chose to shave my head in the shower and rinse it all down the drain. There wasn't a mirror in there, but what the hell! Who knew my head better than I did? It had been attached to my body for as long as I could remember.

I popped in a fresh razor blade, stepped into the shower, dumped some shampoo on my head, and started shaving. The razor slid easily over my scalp, and I was about halfway finished when I noticed several trails of bright red blood running over my chest. By the time I figured out it wasn't a nosebleed, the shower floor was awash in red. Much to my embarrassment, shaving my head using a sharp razor without the aid of a mirror wasn't as easy as I thought it would be. I stepped out of the shower to take a quick peek in the mirror. To my surprise, a dozen small lacerations dotted my scalp! Hell, I couldn't even shave my own head without screwing it up.

As she had done throughout this mess, Jenny came to the rescue. I'm not certain why she didn't take the razor straight to my neck, but in a few minutes she had finished shaving my head with minimal additional blood loss. Grumbling something like "dumbass," she went back downstairs to the kitchen.

Feeling like a fool, I stepped out of the shower, dried off, and looked in the mirror—the same mirror where I'd discovered my inverted nipple months ago.

Staring back at me was a total stranger, completely bald with a dozen razor nicks in his pale, milky scalp and small trickles of blood running down his head. Thin, loose skin formed dark bags under both of his eyes, which were clearly sunken from fatigue. A half-inch-wide scar, healing but still raised and abnormally red, stretched diagonally across his chest from his sternum to his right armpit. Two circular scars, each a half-inch in diameter, sat side by side a few inches below the big one, marking the site of surgical drains.

The skin on this stranger's right side sank in, outlining ribs where the pectoralis muscle should have been. The man in the mirror looked sad, hopeless, and lifeless, as if he were *dying!* For a quick moment I thought of my father; he had the same look a few weeks before he died.

This is serious, I reminded myself. I had the same hopeless feeling I had experienced when I saw my father for the last time.

In my mind I was still a healthy individual who ran every morning, worked sixteen hours a day, and saved lives—not the fading shell of a man who was staring back at me.

Maybe it was fear that brought me back, or possibly my recent conversation with Joan, but as quickly as my out-of-body experience began, it lifted. I pressed my hand against my reflection—against the strange-looking man staring back at me—and told myself the person in the mirror was the real me, the one everyone saw and was concerned about, the one fighting cancer. I needed to join him in the fight. If Joan could take on this disease for fifteen years, I could do the same for a few months.

At that moment I made the decision to take charge of my life, my health, and my emotions. It was time to take stock of who I was and where I was going. Naked, bloody, and bald, I decided cancer wasn't going to take me down mentally or physically. And if it did, I was going to go kicking and screaming. I would make the best of my life and my illness, have fun every chance I could, and help anyone else who would listen. Damn it, I'd make a difference in this crazy, cruel world of cancer. I'd always been up for a challenge, and this one would be no different.

Screw breast cancer! I thought.

This epiphany lifted my spirits. For the first time since I had freaked out while looking in this same mirror just a few short months ago, I had developed an attitude.

"Screw breast cancer, just screw it," I said aloud.

Armed with my new philosophy, I dried off, cleaned up the blood, got dressed, and took another look in the mirror. Damn, my head had a funny shape! There were bumps and ridges I had never seen before, all covered by milky-white, goofy-looking skin. I looked downright weird, but I didn't give a damn. I put on my favorite golf outfit and headed downstairs. The golf course awaited!

Heading down the stairs, though, I had the distinct feeling that I had forgotten my underwear! I stopped and checked. No, my underwear was there, right where it should be, but I still felt half-naked. The sensation was very real, yet absolutely bizarre.

I grabbed my golf clubs and favorite Longhorn baseball cap, opened the garage door, and stepped outside to load the car. As soon as I stepped into the north wind, however, the "no underwear" sensation hit me again. Just to be certain, I checked my fly. It was zipped up all the way, and my underwear was still in place. Then I put on the cap. The damn thing fell down over my eyes and spun around. No matter what I did, it wouldn't stay put.

I had discovered that a full head of hair was absolutely necessary for golf-cap stability. Without hair, the damn thing spun around on my head like a top. I had also lost my head's insulating layer. The cool breeze felt like an Arctic blue norther. Ultraviolet rays are not kind to newly exposed pale skin, either. I never considered slathering sunscreen on my head, but I learned pretty quickly that I needed to. The next day, my scalp was covered with patches of peeling, sunburned skin that just screamed, "I'm not only sick, I'm stupid!"

A week or so after my epiphany in the bathroom, my razor-nicked, sunburned scalp had healed, replaced by smooth, lightly tanned skin. With a little imagination, I envisioned myself as a young

Yul Brynner (minus the chiseled jaw, sex appeal, and stardom). With this look and just a tad more talent, I could have been on Broadway, but fate left me stuck in the operating room.

With a little time, baldness began to appeal to me, but not because of any movie-star fantasy. I'd discovered that a man's newly slick head was absolutely irresistible to the fairer sex. Women couldn't keep their hands off my head, and I loved the attention!

"Alan, I love the new look. Can I rub your head?" I heard it every day.

Because I was on the brink of middle age, the thought of random women rubbing my head was pretty appealing, so I consistently answered that request with an appreciative grin as I tilted my head toward them. A few quick strokes later, they thanked me and said, "That feels good. Weird, but good."

I just grinned. "Come back when you want more."

I soon learned, however, that my new look required maintenance. Slick (definitely not stubble) was the attraction. Although virtually all of my hair was gone, a few random follicles refused to die, requiring a head shave every morning. After a little practice, I could finish in record time, with no blood loss. The time required to keep that slick look was a small price to pay for the new me!

My new look and attitude also made my office even more interesting and fun. Some patients completely ignored my baldness, and some were openly inquisitive. Since I was known to be a little unpredictable, others figured I had just lost a bet.

One patient, however, made my day. Mary was in her early forties, intelligent, outgoing, and always immaculately dressed. She'd been one of my first patients when I started the practice in 1978. I had delivered her kids, who were both teenagers now, and helped her through a few crises along the way. Every year during her annual checkup, we joked, talked about our kids, and caught up on our lives. Medicine entered the conversation only when necessary. She was one of those fascinating women who made the practice of medicine extraordinarily fun and rewarding.

A week into my bald phase, Mary came in for her annual checkup. I sauntered into the exam room and said hello. She squinted at me, focusing on my spit-shined head. Then a startled expression flashed across her face. She was definitely surprised, but she just grinned and said nothing.

I asked about her kids, and she made certain that I noticed the new designer socks she'd worn just for the visit. The word "bald" never crossed her lips during the twenty-minute visit.

"It's good to see you; glad you're doing okay," I said as she left the room.

At the checkout desk, she leaned toward my longtime receptionist, cupped both hands around her mouth and whispered, "I'm really glad Dr. Johns finally got rid of that wig. It never did look natural on him."

Her observation was met with a howl of laughter that resonated through the office. My receptionist finally caught her breath and explained that, first, my hair had been real all those years, and second, it had fallen out because of chemotherapy for breast cancer. Needless to say, Mary was astonished and more than a little embarrassed.

From that day forward, I have initiated every one of her visits with a quick yank on my hair, just to show her that it's real. There's no charge for the added entertainment.

The office amusement and Joan's suggestions helped my attitude immensely, yet my moods at this point remained mercurial. Although my energy level, strength, and attitude were improving, I couldn't ignore the next round of poison that lay ahead of me. The routine was cruel—just as I began to feel human again, it was time for another intravenous bomb to detonate inside my body. The closer the day came, the more irritated and irritable I became, even though I was determined to "screw cancer." I knew exactly what was coming, and nothing short of a lobotomy would help my feelings of dismay. There was no way I could get out of the chemo, and I hated the feeling of being trapped.

For poisoning number three, I arrived at the infusion center in a lousy mood. I crawled into my recliner, offered up my arm, growled something unintelligible to the nurse, plugged in my earphones for a little Willie Nelson, and for the next few hours ignored everything and anyone around me. I was one sour, pissed-off surgeon.

For the first time since early March, I wasn't just mad, I was enraged and infuriated at my situation. There I was, lying in a damn chair, a chunk ripped out of my chest, bald as a bowling ball, and hooked up to an IV with crap pouring into my veins that was going to make me sick as hell for the next seven days. Plus I hated taking Compazine for the nausea. Those damn maroon pills smelled terrible and left me feeling like I was walking around in a half-drunk, half-hung-over, nausea-filled fog.

Shit.

But after a few hours of self-righteous anger, my new "screw cancer" attitude of kicked back in. A bit of venting seemed to give me even more control. I took in my reality and told myself to think only about listening to Willie Nelson and to worry about the next step later on. I did exactly that.

When I left the Infusion Room, I realized that one more bite of the elephant was gone, and I whispered to myself, "Screw breast cancer. I'm a survivor."

CHAPTER TWENTY-ONE

Others

The effects of chemotherapy are cumulative, intensifying with each succeeding round. My treatments were no exception. Despite premedication before being poisoned and mountains of drugs afterward, two weeks following my third round of chemo, I was miserable, lethargic, and chronically nauseated.

I was requiring more and more recovery time. When Round Four approached, I was still seasick from Round Three and more than a little depressed at the prospect of lying in that damn infusion chair again.

One night when I couldn't sleep, I aimed my magic wand at the elephant, dreamed up a few voodoo chants, and tried zapping it out of existence. I commanded the wand to bring a premature end to my misery, but nothing changed. A nice chunk of the elephant was still there.

Tequila didn't help either.

What kept me going was to focus on what was happening to me and why. I was lucky because I understood what was happening in my body and why it needed to happen, but most patients don't.

Every organ in our bodies contains millions of cells that constantly reproduce and grow. Some cells (e.g. hair, bone marrow, and the intestinal tract lining) grow very rapidly. Others (e.g. bone, skin, and muscle) reproduce very slowly. Cancer cells generally grow much more rapidly than normal tissue, and chemotherapy attacks the tissue that is growing most rapidly—usually the cancer.

Unfortunately, chemotherapy medicines cannot tell the difference between cancer cells and normal cells. As a result, normal cells are killed off along with cancer cells, and the effect on both types of cells is cumulative with each successive dose. The trick is to destroy more cancer than normal tissue, and that requires maintaining a delicate balance between too much and too little poison.

I found it more and more difficult to recover after each chemo round and was always tempted to quit or delay the upcoming dose. Yet I knew that doing so would sabotage my ultimate goal of being cured, and I certainly didn't want to die of metastatic breast cancer.

The fact that I could die was emphasized two weeks after my third poisoning. I felt terrible, and the constant undercurrent of nausea was punctuated by a burning in my stomach that could only be relieved by a continuous dose of peanut butter. Unfortunately, peanut butter accentuated my thirst, and drinking water exaggerated the nausea. I sat at my desk one morning feeling pretty sorry for myself in this cancer catch-22.

My private office was spacious and comfortable, with floor-to-ceiling windows covering the northwest wall. The windows afforded a great view of the office parking area and the outside world. It was a great place to sit and contemplate my life.

At seven-thirty one morning I was sick as a dog. I stared at the ominous clouds rolling in, blotting out what was left of the sunny morning. The weather seemed to be teaming up with my stomach to maximize misery. As if to emphasize the point, a stray dog backed up to the window, looked at me, and relieved himself right on the window. Neither the magic wand nor my "screw breast cancer" attitude could lift the oppressive fog that had enveloped me that morning.

Theresa, my loyal nurse for fifteen years, walked into the office, handed me the first patient's chart, and said, "Come on, it's time to start. And get ready—it's not good." Her words immediately broke my fog because her voice had cracked a little; she was obviously disturbed by what she had seen.

I stood and walked into the first exam room.

Peggy had been my patient for as long as Theresa had been my nurse. I'd delivered her daughter, Paige, fourteen years ago and had seen Peggy yearly ever since. The last time I had seen her, she'd been a vibrant, healthy, and physically active woman who enjoyed snow skiing every winter with her husband and Paige. The conversation during that visit was dominated by talk of the ski trip her family had planned for December 1997.

Despite Theresa's warning, I was totally unprepared for the scene that confronted me as I entered the exam room. Peggy sat in a chair in the far corner of the room. Her eyes spoke volumes. Lifeless, hopeless, and sunken, they were surrounded by thin, almost translucent pale skin through which I could see small blood vessels. She was completely bald and unbelievably thin, having lost fifty pounds since I last saw her. A red blouse covered her shoulders but could not hide her skeletal appearance. She was a mere shell of the woman I had seen the year before.

Looking worried and afraid, Paige sat in the chair next to her mom.

I took a seat across from them, and Peggy explained what had happened. Her once strong voice was soft but still determined.

Their ski vacation had been uneventful until she took a pretty benign fall on a gentle, groomed slope. The pain in her back was instantaneous and incapacitating. After a short trip down the mountain with the ski patrol, an emergency room visit, and an MRI, she was told what was wrong.

The doctors found several collapsed vertebra in her lower back, all of which were infiltrated with tumor. Metastatic cancer had weakened her vertebral bones to the point that a low-speed fall into a soft snow bank had crushed them.

After a quick flight back to Fort Worth and a complete evaluation, she was given the diagnosis: a very small breast cancer had already spread to her spine, ribs, liver, and brain. *With* aggressive chemotherapy and radiation, she had six to nine months, maybe.

She had endured six months of chemotherapy and radiation regimens that made what I was going through look like a vacation in Maui. Despite these desperate and physically devastating attempts to control her disease, the cancer had progressed. There was nothing further to be done. She was meeting with hospice in a few days and was in the process of preparing for the inevitable.

I was speechless and tried to absorb what had happened when she came to the point of the visit.

"Dr. Johns, you've helped me through a lot of things over the last fifteen years, and I trust your judgment, but now I really need reassurance. I know I'm not going to be around for Paige, but I want to be certain that she won't face what's happening to me. You delivered her, and she trusts you. I want you to promise to do everything you can to help her avoid what has happened to me."

Paige's tearful eyes were full of fear, uncertainty, even terror, but she said nothing.

I had spent the last twenty-eight years learning the science of medicine and surgery, but nothing had prepared me for this.

I had no answer for Peggy's medical problems, but I had one for Paige.

Composing myself, I looked at Peggy and said, "I promise I'll do everything I can to help her." I wasn't sure what that would be, but I meant it. A few moments later we said our goodbyes and the visit was over.

Back in my office, misery about my own circumstances melted away as I watched them walk back to their car, hand in hand.

I never saw Peggy again.

Those brief few moments transformed me. The fog, self-pity, and melancholy I'd been feeling thirty minutes earlier were gone, never to return. Despite my procrastination about going to the doctor when I was face-to-face with a life-threatening illness, I still had a great chance to survive, but Peggy didn't. My surgery and chemotherapy had been a small price to pay for survival, and I sure as hell should be thankful for both.

The squirrel cage in my brain spun incessantly all afternoon. I wasn't certain how I would keep my promise to Peggy, but, by damn, I would.

Round Four of my poisoning regimen came the following Friday. This time I was fully doped up before walking in, and I remember very little about it. According to the infusion nurse, I climbed in the lounge chair, laughed, and said, "Give me a small order of the Red Devil and a couple of pints of the clear stuff. And put it on my tab."

Four down, two to go.

By Tuesday, I was back in the office, still wondering what I could do for Paige.

Midmorning, I heard, "Dr. Johns, line one." After picking up the phone, I was greeted with, "Hi, Alan. I heard you're doing great."

It was Ralph, the railroad-spike-wielding radiologist who had done my first biopsy.

"Yeah, I'm fine," I lied, trying not to heave. Just the sound of his voice made my chest hurt.

"I just saw a patient of yours, Linda A. She's got a spot in her left breast, and it's not good."

I recognized the name of my longtime patient immediately.

"Thanks, Ralph. I'll call her."

I became Linda's doctor in 1980, when she was twenty-one. At five feet ten, slender, with a dark complexion, long black hair, and captivating, beautiful blue eyes, she was a striking woman. Her smile and personality simply exuded enthusiasm. She'd been married barely two months when I'd found tumors in both of her ovaries.

She and her new husband had been terrified by the possibilities that lay ahead of them: surgery, loss of both ovaries, and no chance for a family. Gynecological ultrasound was in its infancy, so I had very few tools with which to evaluate the masses, but it was evident she needed surgery. I told Linda and her husband I would do everything possible to save the ovaries and, I hoped, their chances of having a family.

Surgery went well, both tumors were benign, and I was able to salvage a small portion of each ovary. I felt quite proud of myself when, with a little medical help, Linda became pregnant about eighteen months later. I delivered her only child, a son, in 1982.

A recurrent tumor required me to remove the remainder of one ovary a few years later, and she was never able to have another child, becoming prematurely menopausal about ten years later, at age thirty-three. All this raced through my mind as Ralph spoke.

After I hung up with Ralph, I processed what he'd told me. I had to call her, but I hesitated because now I knew what it was like to be on the receiving end of one of these calls. Before my diagnosis, my routine had been to call patients and ask them to come in. This allowed me to give them their diagnosis face-to-face and answer questions. Now, however, I knew how terrifying that simple phone call could be. But I had to make it.

Linda picked up the phone on the third ring, and I asked her to come into the office to talk. She and her husband arrived that afternoon about two. She was now thirty-nine years old and her son was sixteen. For the second time in two weeks, I faced a longtime patient who had to be given devastating news, and this time I was the person delivering it.

Amid their tears, I explained exactly what she would be going through during the next few weeks. Emphasizing that her tumor was early-stage and very curable, I tried to be optimistic, but I knew that all they heard were the words "breast cancer."

Since I was completely bald and moderately green from nausea, I might not have been very reassuring to them, but they left the office armed with reasonably accurate knowledge of what was to come and some reasons for optimism.

I reported for my fifth round of chemotherapy the same few days later that Linda had a mastectomy and sentinel node identification in Fort Worth. Sentinel node technology was new to our city, but several surgeons were offering it.

Her sentinel node was negative, so no axillary dissection was done, and chemotherapy wasn't thought to be necessary. After a few months of radiation, she was finished with her treatment.

She was the first patient that I had taken from diagnosis through treatment since my own breast cancer diagnosis. Helping her through the maze was as fulfilling as anything I had accomplished in my medical career (with the possible exception of trading triplets for a Harley-Davidson).

During the next few months, I began to guide other patients through the process, both personally (with support and explanations) and professionally (to make sure they got the best care and advice available.)

For the next three years, Linda and I spent most of her annual checkups talking about her son and comparing war stories about mammograms, mastectomies, and doctors. Everything seemed great.

Until it wasn't.

Four years after her surgery, she developed a persistent headache. Routine treatment didn't help, so we did an MRI. The results were shocking and sobering: metastatic breast cancer in her liver, ribs, and brain. Intensive monthly chemotherapy kept the disease at bay for a while, but with her son and husband at her bedside, she died at home in 2004, at age forty-five.

Obviously her sentinel node hadn't really been negative; maybe it hadn't been correctly identified, or maybe it was just bad luck. Regardless, the identification process had made no difference whatsoever, because her outcome was the same as Peggy's.

In the next few years, I saw at least a dozen patients with the same story and the same end result as Linda and Peggy.

By early 2003 I had developed a strong connection with my patients who were fighting breast cancer as well as those who had lost the battle. My frustration at my inability to provide more-effective support and guidance for them had reached a crescendo.

Joan, Linda, Peggy, and Paige had become the foundation for my quest for solutions to this problem. As much pain and fear as my cancer had put me through, without it I would not have gained the knowledge and experience I needed to make a difference in the world of breast cancer. Sometimes good things really do emerge from bad ones.

Before my breast cancer diagnosis, I had not been aware of the degree to which breast cancer treatment protocols varied among surgeons. I had sent my patients to excellent surgeons without really understanding the issues they were to face. More importantly, I had little concept of the importance of whom my patients saw and what those doctors did. I had burrowed very deeply into my own little corner of the medical world.

But with my breast cancer experience, I began to understand how disjointed the care for breast cancer patients actually was. The care could be excellent but totally without coordination, at least from the patient's standpoint. A patient was sent first to the radiologist, then the surgeon, then the oncologist, then the radiation oncologist, and finally the plastic surgeon. These doctors were invariably scattered all over the city and rarely talked to one another about the patient's case unless the presentation was so unusual that it demanded early cooperation. Patients rarely had the advantage of all the different specialists getting together to discuss their individual cases *before* anything was done.

As the years went by, I saw more and more patients die of metastatic disease when they supposedly had small tumors and negative nodes. Even though this happens in the best of circumstances, the importance of a comprehensive approach to every patient was becoming obvious.

. . .

But back in 1999, I was blissfully ignorant of what lay ahead for Linda. I was just happy to be in a position to help her understand what was happening and why. My experiences in medical school and residency had begun my transformation from student to physician, and my encounter with breast cancer had been an education unto itself, but I had a lot more to learn before I could efficiently and effectively merge my patient and physician roles. My experience with Linda had been the beginning of that process.

My sixth and final appointment with the Red Devil, Adriamycin, was only a few days away, and the anticipation of finally having the awful chemotherapy behind me was palpable. For the first time since this all began, I was truly excited as I drove to the cancer center. We were to meet with Dr. N before the last tortuous bout began.

Dr. N's glossy scalp reflected the florescent lights in the ceiling above his desk. I chuckled under my breath, wondering what my new hair would look like when it started growing back in a few weeks.

Dr. N held my latest blood work report in his left hand. My blood had been drawn a few minutes earlier in preparation for my last dose of chemotherapy, which was scheduled to begin in about an hour.

"Alan, your white count is pretty low," he said.

He was referring to my white blood cell count. White blood cells fight infection and are constantly being produced by bone marrow. Like cancer cells, they are produced very rapidly. Too much chemotherapy can kill them off, leaving a person extremely susceptible to infection and with no effective mechanism to fight it off.

I'm pretty certain my response to Dr. N was, "Shit! Now what?"

"Ideally, we might delay your last chemo treatment for a couple of weeks to let your count build back up," he said.

Since I was physically and psychologically ready for the last dose, nothing could have been more disappointing. The thought of waiting another two weeks suddenly became intolerable.

With resolute determination that was obvious to Dr. N, I let loose. "You said *might*, not *must*, so let's just do it and cope with whatever happens afterwards. My fatigue, nausea, fear, anxiety, and anger have become almost overwhelming, and I've got to get this last damn dose done. This absolutely, positively has to be over with today!"

Then I took a breath.

"Okay, fine," he said, not wanting to push the issue.

As I walked into the Infusion Room, it seemed as if someone had pulled back all the curtains. Sunlight filled the room, the nurses were smiling, and the patients seemed happy, too. It was as if everyone knew it was my last chemo.

A few hours later, poisoning number six was over. I thanked the nurses, gave every patient a hug and an encouraging pat on the back, and walked out with a huge grin plastered all over my face. I even stopped at the reception desk to thank the grizzly-bear-wrestling, hundred-page-form-handling receptionist. She let out a barely audible growl as I headed out the door.

The sense of relief I carried to the car that afternoon is indescribable. Despite being the world's biggest dumbass with an MD after his name, my torture was over and I had survived.

Within a week of my last date with the Red Devil, I was on a world-class high. Every cell in my brain released the endorphins they had been hoarding during the previous few months. That endorphin rush produced feelings that offset the worst of the symptoms that had plagued me.

Most, but not all. As soon as I could look at a medium-rare rib eye with ravenous lust instead of fleeting nausea, I would really be ready to move on.

Nearly all cancer patients experience similar cathartic emotions with the last chemotherapy, the last surgery, the last radiation treatment, or, most often, the removal of their portacath. Whatever the event, it becomes a highly symbolic end to the most wretched phase of a cancer patient's life, and I was there.

Physicians occasionally suggest that the portacath be left in place, just in case the cancer returns and more treatment becomes necessary. Most docs have no clue about the implications of that recommendation. No matter how medically reasonable it is, the patient only hears, "Your cancer may come back, and we might need to do this again," and that is a depressing, bone-chilling thought.

Among a host of other things, my cancer experience has taught me that not removing a portacath as soon after the last chemo dose as possible tells a patient that she *might* not be finished. This implicit suggestion can suck the hope out of anyone. Just get rid of the damn thing—it can always be replaced easily and quickly.

I have learned to be honest and direct, but I have never forgotten how downright ecstatic I felt at the saga's end. Patients should never be deprived of that feeling; it's an incredibly important part of the recovery process. Replacing the port is easy; seeing no end to the treatment, even only symbolically, is devastating.

The morning after my last round of chemo, I awoke with one overriding thought: *It's finally over.* The emotion was one of overwhelming liberation. No more headaches, nausea, fatigue, and feeling like crap. No more mounds of pills just to survive another poisoning, no more nightly dates with the porcelain throne, and no more IVs. My hair might come back, too, though I really enjoyed being bald.

My next appointment with Dr. N was six weeks away. I had plenty of time to recover and get my life back. The end of this train ride to hell was near.

Or so I thought.

CHAPTER TWENTY-TWO

Hot Flashes?

After six long months of chemo, I'd finally received my last dose of the Red Devil. Afterward, I walked out of the Infusion Room a happy and victorious man. A few weeks later I began to feel somewhat human again.

The previous six months had been the most miserable of my fifty years, both physically and mentally. Without Jenny's support, care, and patience, and the constant psychological lift my daughters provided, I probably would have just said, "To hell with it all."

During their treatment, cancer patients tend to be angry, indifferent, hateful, demanding, and generally unpleasant to those closest to them. Although we are the ones with cancer, and treatment has become our own personal hellhole, our families and friends usually find themselves directly downhill from, and on the receiving end of, the misery-coated crap we often dish out. I knew my family deserved better treatment than that, but they rarely got it from me.

When I began feeling like my old self, Jenny realized that everyone needed a break. A frozen margarita on a sunny Mexican beach sounded great to me, so we flew to Cancun for a short "get out of town, it's over, let your hair grow back" vacation.

The end of my chemotherapy was a significant milestone for all of us, and I wanted to celebrate with my family. The trip was a way to bring all of us together and for me to say thanks, apologize for being an occasional ass, and not mention breast cancer even once.

In Cancun, food tasted great for the first time in months. The beach was spectacular, the margaritas were excellent, and the four of us were able to recapture the relaxation, conversation, and laughter that had always defined our family. Finally we could leave the horrendous last six months behind us.

Late one afternoon I sat on the beach alone, staring out at the Gulf. *It's over, it's really over,* I thought. Yet even in this euphoric state, on a pristine beach with an immaculate sunset on the horizon and my third Patrón Añejo margarita on the rocks (gently shaken, with salt and lime) resting comfortably in my hand, I couldn't keep my mind from wandering back to Peggy and the others who had lost their lives to breast cancer. I was here, alive and celebrating, but there would be no celebratory trips for them or their families.

The unfairness of their situations burned in my chest. Thoughts about them kept the squirrel cage in my mind spinning constantly.

That late afternoon on the beach, with the sun plunging behind the ocean, I promised myself I was going to do something positive about breast cancer treatment in Fort Worth. I didn't know how, when, or where, but I knew that if I set this as my goal, I'd achieve it.

A few days later my family and I returned to Fort Worth. My tanned, bowling-ball head was beginning to sprout some serious stubble, making me look like a human Chia Pet. It was time to make a decision. I needed to commit to shaving my head every day to maintain the Telly Savalas look or let my hair grow back, one or the other. I opted for hair because I was particularly curious to see if it would come in as thick as before. Everyone assured me it would, but after what I'd been through, I didn't believe everyone anymore.

By the time I returned to Dr. N's office for my first post-treatment visit, I was sporting a new growth of thick, reddish-brown hair. Jenny and I were in a great mood as we sat in Dr. N's office and patiently waited for our poison-wielding, bald-headed friend to grace us with his presence.

While waiting, I noticed something peculiar. A distinctive noxious odor had been bothering me since I'd walked through the building's front door. It was as if I could smell Adriamycin and Cytoxan, but I knew that was ridiculous—those drugs are odorless. Regardless, something was assaulting my nose and making me more nauseated by the moment.

Later I figured out what was going on. The faint but unmistakable smell of Dr. N's office triggered a Pavlovian conditioned response—my nausea. As soon as I left his office, I was fine. To this day, I can't sit in that office without developing a twinge of nausea.

That day Jenny and I had to wait an hour for Dr. N. During our wait, she and I thoroughly and repetitively studied every one of his diplomas, which adorned the walls of that tiny office. Finally Dr. N waltzed in and sat at his desk, seemingly oblivious to the time we'd been kept waiting. For just a moment I thought that if I weren't a doctor, I might really dislike physicians because we often give the impression that we are arrogant pricks, even to each other.

After a few niceties, Dr. N got to the point. Only then did I understand why he'd waited as long as humanly possible before coming in to talk with us.

"Alan, I'm recommending that you take Tamoxifen for five years."

I startled, then stared at him. I couldn't have been more surprised if he'd walked in wearing a black leather skirt and heels. I'd known Dr. N for years, and I trusted him, but his suggestion made no sense. My nodes were negative, I'd survived chemotherapy, and I thought the train wreck that had been my life for the past year was finally over. Why the hell would I need any more medicine?

I don't recall overreacting to his suggestion, but Jenny swears I did. I thought I used my best doctor voice, careful not to imply that I was questioning him in any way.

Jenny claims that everyone in the building heard me.

"Just what the *hell* are you talking about?" I asked.

At that time, the drug Dr. N wanted me to take, Tamoxifen, had recently been approved by the Food and Drug Administration. Some of my patients were on it, and I knew it was an estrogen-receptor modulator. Breast cells (as well as uterine and vaginal cells) have receptors on their surfaces. Estrogen binds with these receptors like one piece of a jigsaw puzzle fitting perfectly with another. Once estrogen joins a receptor on the cell wall, a chemical reaction is triggered within the cell that causes it to grow and reproduce.

If a patient takes Tamoxifen, however, the drug binds to these estrogen receptors on the cells but doesn't activate them. The idea is to "clog up" all of the estrogen receptors with Tamoxifen, leaving none to interact with estrogen, thus blocking estrogen's effect and keeping the cells from growing.

Most breast cancer cells require estrogen to reproduce, and estrogen-receptor-positive breast cancers are very common. As long as a breast cancer patient takes Tamoxifen, the estrogen receptors on the surface of their cancer cells stay blocked, and the cancer doesn't grow. Eventually the cancer cells die. By their very nature, however, cancer cells are chromosomally bizarre and unpredictable. Some cancer cells may not do what we expect them to do, so Tamoxifen is not a guarantee that the cancer won't surface again.

My mind began to spin: *After all that poison, Dr. N thinks there still might be die-hard clusters of breast cancer cells hiding behind my pancreas,*

between my ribs, or in some deep hidden recess of my body, just lying in
wait for the opportunity to grow!

I knew how Tamoxifen worked in women, but I had no idea what
it did to men. Turns out, neither did Dr. N.

"Do you have any idea how Tamoxifen will help me?" I asked
after calming down a bit.

"A big study was just published that demonstrated Tamoxifen
would decrease the chances of breast cancer coming back by 5
to 10 percent; therefore, it might lower your chances of dying of
the disease."

All I could think about was my patient Peggy. Suddenly a
scrawny, 125-pound version of *me* flashed before my eyes.

"But you're talking about how it affects women. What about
men?" I managed to ask.

He shook his head. "Beats me, but if it works for women, it should
do the same for you." He looked over the top of his glasses. Beads of
sweat were forming on his shiny head. Obviously this was a difficult
conversation for him, too. "Alan, your cancer is HER2/neu positive,
estrogen and progesterone receptor positive, grade two, and the
tumor measured over one centimeter in diameter. None of those
are particularly favorable parameters. I think Tamoxifen could do
you some good." (HER2/neu is a type of receptor involved in many
breast cancers.)

"But do you have any idea what the side effects would be for
me?" I asked, struggling to get used to the idea.

"It causes hot flashes in women, but I have no idea about men. I
don't know any men who have taken it."

Now *that* was certainly reassuring.

I was crushed, stunned, pissed, and scared all at once. I had
just been through surgery (which I was certain had cured me) and
chemotherapy (just in case the surgery hadn't), and now Dr. N

wanted me to take a pill every day for the next five years! And he had no idea what it would do to me!

I was ready for my illness to be over with so I could move on. Somehow, taking a pill every day for the next 1,826 days didn't seem like moving on.

I was also stunned because the possibility of my cancer recurring hadn't crossed my mind—avoiding that was what chemotherapy had been all about. I had repressed even a scintilla of that idea. But in Dr. N's office, I began to understand what the term "living with cancer" really meant.

Dr. N removed his glasses, wiped both lenses with a Kleenex, repositioned them, wiped his head with the same Kleenex, cleared his throat, and looked at me again. Obviously he wasn't finished.

"I also want you to consider radiation therapy, daily for six weeks."

That one freaked me out big-time. Just the word *radiation* brought back visions of dozens of patients I had seen during my residency. They all had incurable cervical or rectal cancer and had been treated with radium pellets inserted into their tumors. Radiation emitted from the pellets turned their tumors, and the surrounding tissue, into an ulcerated, bloody mess that exuded an odor worse than anything I had ever experienced. These poor folks died anyway, but the treatment doomed them to suffer with huge necrotic holes in their bodies that never healed.

Based on my limited experience many years ago, I had concluded that radiation was bad and was used for people with *real* cancer who were going to die anyway. I know that these assumptions were simpleminded (particularly for a doctor), but we're all tainted by our experiences, and radiation therapy carried horrible connotations in my mind.

Dr. N quickly figured out what I was thinking. He and I knew radiation therapy had improved dramatically in the past twenty years and was infinitely better and safer in 1999, but that mattered little to me because I couldn't erase the memories.

My reasoning wasn't totally irrational, however. In my case, radiation would simply be used to decrease the chance of breast cancer coming back in the skin around my surgical scar, but it would have no effect on whether I survived or not. Combined with this rationale, emotion won out.

"No radiation," I said forcefully. "If I get a skin cancer recurrence, I'll cope with it then!"

Quietly sitting to my right during this entire exchange, Jenny had endured the conversation as long as she could.

"All right, you two, stop all this nonsense. I'm tired of listening, and y'all haven't accomplished a blessed thing. Dr. N, just tell us what you would do if you were sitting on our side of this damn desk." Jenny doesn't tolerate unproductive BS well.

Dr. N looked a little startled, but he quickly composed himself. "Okay, here's the deal. Tamoxifen decreases the risk of recurrence by 5 to 10 percent in women, so it should be the same for men. I won't argue with you about the radiation, but I think you should take the Tamoxifen."

I looked at Jenny. She was losing her patience. Just before she gets pissed, she always stops talking and curls her right eyebrow down a bit. The eyebrow was definitely curled down.

"Just take the damn pills, Alan. It's not that hard." Then her eyebrow came back up.

My decision came quickly. Considering the 10 percent advantage *and* a happy wife, I reached over the desk and shook Dr. N's hand, thanked him for his help and advice, and asked for a prescription. Once I thought about the options, the decision was deceivingly simple. I'd take the damn pill every day. How hard could that be? After all, only another 1,825 days would remain after I took the first one!

Back home we had dinner, played with Harley, and I took my first pill. I was pleasantly surprised that nothing happened. I felt nothing that night, the next morning, or the next few days. I was beginning to feel a little foolish for even thinking about not taking the Tamoxifen.

But four days later and with 1,821 pills to go, all that changed.

Thursday, March 11, 1999

After finishing my 5:30 a.m. run, I showered, dressed for the office, petted the dog, kissed the wife, and headed out for my Richland Hills office. From my first day in private practice, I had worked out of two offices, one adjacent to the Fort Worth downtown hospital, the other in Richland Hills, a northeastern suburb of Fort Worth. That office was a thirty-minute drive from our house.

I rolled down the window to enjoy the beautiful, crisp morning. I felt more alive than I'd felt in years. I was wearing a new, light blue dress shirt and sedate burgundy tie that Jenny and the kids had given me as a "finished cancer, back to work" gift.

About three miles from home, just as I gunned my little Jeep SUV down the access road toward Interstate 30, my face began to burn like I'd spent the last twelve hours staring directly into the sun. Simultaneously, every hair follicle on my head and arms stood straight up, as if I'd walked into a freezer. My arms, face, neck, and chest were covered with goose bumps. Before reaching the end of the ramp, my forehead, chest, and armpits broke out in a profuse sweat. Soon my shirt was soaked and I looked like I'd just run through a spring rainstorm without an umbrella.

By the time I managed to pull off the highway onto the shoulder, the event was over and I felt fine. All I could think was, *What the hell just happened to me?*

My reflection in the mirror was startling. My face was beet-red and slick with sweat, yet I felt fine. As a doctor, and not thinking about how being a patient *and* a doctor had worked out for me so far, I thought I knew exactly what had happened: Obviously the sweating episode was caused by my morning run. I hadn't taken enough time to cool down. That was totally reasonable—maybe not rational, but reasonable. And the explanation made more and more sense as I drove the few miles back home. By the time I pulled into the garage, I was certain that was what had just happened. Tomorrow I'd just take a little more time to cool down. That would fix the problem. Satisfied, I changed clothes and drove to the office.

My day was uneventful until 3:00 p.m. I was in the middle of a conversation with Francine, a long-term patient in her mid-fifties, about her two teenage kids. Suddenly I felt as if someone had placed a sunlamp about three inches from my chest. Within a few seconds the heat rose, traversed my back, pulsed into my neck, and set my face on fire. My arms broke out in goose bumps again as a cold sweat covered my face, puddled under my arms, and ran down my chest. Moments later, another shirt was soaked.

This isn't good.

The squirrel cage in my head kicked into overdrive. Intermittent, violent sweating episodes can be a sign of lymphoma, tuberculosis, and a host of other diseases. The entire litany of possibilities ran through my mind in a few seconds, as more sweat covered my forehead and began to run into my eyes. *Crap, first cancer and now lymphoma.* I had already diagnosed myself.

I was about to excuse myself from the exam room when Francine spoke up.

"Dr. Johns, are you having a hot flash?" Sometimes a patient can be smarter than her doctor. "I'm just asking because your face is beet-red and you're sweating like crazy. It's no big deal; I have them all the time," she said as the next flush worked its way up my neck.

The Tamoxifen!

If a dumbass vaccine existed, I needed a quick dose. I didn't have lymphoma or some exotic infectious disease. I was having medicine-induced hot flashes, the same kind that plagued so many of my patients as they approached menopause. The same ones I had secretly thought couldn't possibly be as bad as my patients had claimed. And the same ones I had found so damnably difficult and frustrating to treat.

I dabbed sweat from my eyelids and looked at Francine. Just as suddenly as it raged through my body, the flush subsided. "I'll bet it just went away; they don't last long," she said with a reassuring tone.

"I'm sure your diagnosis is right," I sheepishly admitted, then explained I was taking Tamoxifen. Then another flush hit and she started laughing uncontrollably.

"I'm sorry, Dr. Johns. I'm not laughing at your breast cancer, but it's hilarious that you've been blessed with the same hot flashes that plague us. It seems only fair," she said between giggles.

I had to agree as another hot flash crawled up my neck.

June 1999

Fort Worth is a pretty large city, so I was amazed at how rapidly word of my hot flash "dilemma" got around. My unpredictable, middle-of-the-exam, try-not-to-drip-sweat-on-a-patient's-belly hot flashes quickly became legendary among my menopausal patients. Almost every one of them greeted me with, "How are your flashes, Doc?" And that was usually followed by, "Had your mammogram this year? Don't worry, it's just a little pressure!"

I was living "The Revenge of the Menopausal Patient" and loving it; you would hear no complaints from me. In spite of my procrastination, modern medicine had saved my life. In the process, the fear that had plagued me, the painful surgery I had endured, the nausea-producing chemotherapy, and the continual hot flashes had combined to produce a different gynecologist than I had been before "the lump." And I was thrilled with the evolution.

You see, my cancer experience melded with my medical school education, residency training, and practical experience to evolve me into a doctor who was on a quest to make sure all breast cancer patients would be treated fairly and properly. I finally understood *fully* what it's like to be a patient and have a physician treat me with the dignity and respect that all human beings deserve.

My journey had also exposed the despicable hodgepodge that faced most breast cancer patients: a disjointed system that they were required to navigate almost entirely by themselves, with little help from my profession.

Combined with my background in research and science, my brush with breast cancer had transformed me into a rabidly passionate advocate of evidence-based medicine and an avowed enemy of "snake-oil" pseudomedicine and its practitioners, who so often take advantage of cancer patients by promising them a "natural" cure with no side effects. All they need is some money.

Fueled by the fact that my knowledge and connections had allowed me to navigate my own treatment and take shortcuts to the best care medicine had to offer, I was sympathetic with patients who had no such advantages. I realized that hour-long waiting room experiences and mountains of paperwork could be avoidable. The unfairness of all this spurred me on, and I was hell-bent on changing the system. I became a man possessed, inspired to make sure breast cancer patients were offered the same high-quality care that had saved my life.

During the next 1,719 days, every one of my approximately 8,595 hot flashes reminded me of my vow to correct this very flawed system, and I began searching for a way to do so. I didn't know how I was going to begin, but I remained determined.

This quest had begun with my promise to Paige and her mother. Then Linda died. I saw her in my office only a couple of months before she passed away, and it was heartbreaking. I then began to be very public about my disease, speaking at several Susan G. Komen functions, Reach to Recovery forums, and one international gynecological meeting where I was the keynote speaker.

With all this exposure, I was seeing newly diagnosed breast cancer patients in my office every couple of weeks. They were looking for help and direction to navigate through the system.

I realized that this onslaught had to stop. After talking with Dr. Marilyn L on several occasions, the facts became obvious: Fort Worth, the twentieth-largest city in the United States, needed a comprehensive breast center to bring together and integrate all the specialists and support staff that are required to effectively treat breast cancer patients using evidence-based guidelines.

An earlier attempt to initiate this type of program into the large, 650-bed hospital where I'd been practicing for twenty years had been met with resounding yawns. Joan (the wonderful woman who brought me the magic wand and elephant) and I continued helping as many women as we could within a complicated, mazelike, incomplete system; however, more and more women were contacting us, and it was becoming overwhelming.

Jenny and I had talked about this for several years. We knew that Fort Worth needed a facility where women could go for this integrated medical service, but we had neither the funds nor the place to start a program, so we continued to help as many women as we could. We both wondered many times where in the world could we get enough money for the dream.

In the meantime, I continued to work and take my daily Tamoxifen. Finally, in 2004 Jenny and I celebrated my last Tamoxifen tablet (one thousand, seven hundred and eighteen of the damn things) with a couple of medium-rare rib eyes and a fine bottle of cabernet. I embraced each remaining hot flash with gusto; the last one came two weeks later. It was the honest-to-goodness, real-deal, no-more-of-this-crap finale. It was finally over.

After discovering my breast tumor and enduring biopsies, mammograms, a mastectomy, chemotherapy, five years of drugs, flushes, and more mammograms, my journey as a fifty-plus male gynecologist with breast cancer had finally ended. But because of Peggy, Paige, Joan, Linda, and the hundreds of other breast cancer patients I now knew, my *real* quest was just beginning.

Epilogue

By December 2002, my physicians' group had grown to sixty doctors representing eight specialties, including twenty OB-GYNs. We all practiced out of the same 650-bed hospital in Fort Worth where I'd tried earlier to arouse some interest in developing a comprehensive breast center. That effort had been for naught.

I continued speaking with newly diagnosed breast cancer patients every week, either in my office or at home. Every person I spoke with was as terrified as I had been, and each needed help, hope, and direction.

Through her volunteer and philanthropic work with numerous breast cancer organizations, Joan had become the face of breast cancer in Fort Worth. She also had been inundated with daily phone calls from frantic breast cancer patients seeking her advice and encouragement.

Fort Worth was now the seventeenth-largest city in the U.S. Given the prevalence of breast cancer, the fact that we did not have an integrated, comprehensive, patient-centered, state-of-the-art breast center where patients could go for medical, social, and psychological support was astounding and embarrassing.

Even though it was 2002, when it came to breast cancer, Fort Worth was still mired in the old-school way of doing things: The patient had a biopsy, and a few days later she got a phone call informing her she had breast cancer. Then she was sent to a surgeon, who might not have spoken to the person who did the biopsy. After surgery, she was directed to an oncologist, who most likely didn't speak with the surgeon, and then to a plastic surgeon, who usually had never spoken to any of the other doctors. After surgery and reconstruction, the patient might be directed to a radiation center across town; the doctors there might not have communicated with her other doctors.

To make matters worse, if the patient required a full axillary node dissection, she was likely to have lymphedema—her arm and hand would swell with fluid. Although it's not horribly painful, this condition is debilitating and almost impossible to treat, and it *is* impossible to cure. So she would need to find someone, anyone, who would help her with a lymphedematous arm that had swollen to the size of a tree trunk.

It was also rare for physicians to get together as a group to discuss a patient *before* a treatment regimen was suggested. Such a discussion might occur for an unusual medical situation or if the patient had advanced disease, but "routine" cases were rarely, if ever, discussed. (If you get cancer of any kind, I doubt you will consider it "routine.")

Patients were handed off from one doc to the next as if they were rolling down a Detroit auto assembly line, hoping like hell they would drop off the end and "drive away" with as good a chance of a cure as possible.

But by 2002, modern treatment for breast cancer was rapidly evolving into an extremely individualized and complex series of decisions, and coordination and discussion among the different specialists was becoming more and more advantageous.

The more knowledgeable I became about this situation, the

more I was determined to change it; however, my goal turned out to be harder to achieve than I had expected.

My continued suggestion that Fort Worth needed a comprehensive breast center usually met with a curt, "Everything seems to be going just fine; we just don't see the need," followed by a complimentary, "Thanks for your suggestion. We'll look into it some other time." But some other time never came.

I was desolate but not beaten. And just when I thought my goal was hopeless, an opportunity arose in 2003, when the Baylor Healthcare System decided to build a state-of-the-art women's hospital in downtown Fort Worth. My OB-GYN group was approached to participate in the design and governance of the new women's hospital, which was slated to open in 2008. Less than a nanosecond later, my partners and I agreed to participate. We knew this was the professional chance of a lifetime. We would be instrumental in the design, construction, and governance of a women's specialty hospital where we could proudly finish our careers.

Almost immediately the squirrel cage in my mind fired up again. Why couldn't the hospital also have a comprehensive breast center?

After numerous meetings with the All Saints Health Foundation (the organization that would be responsible for raising the funds for the women's hospital) and the new hospital administration, the concept of a comprehensive breast center at Baylor's Andrews Women's Hospital was officially conceived in March 2005.

For the first two years, only Jenny, the administrator of the new hospital, the foundation director, and I knew about the breast center concept. It took a Herculean effort to get the general surgeons on board. I knew it would. Most doctors (myself included) want no part of anything they perceive as interfering with their ways of practicing medicine. And I was savvy enough to know that if I couldn't get the doctors to agree, the plans for the breast center would fall apart.

For a year and a half, the director of the foundation, the CEO of the hospital, and I met every two months with about fifteen breast cancer patients from the Bosom Buddies, a group of breast cancer survivors who got together every month for lunch. Many of these women had left Fort Worth and gone elsewhere for their breast cancer care.

Our reason for meeting with them was simple. We needed to know what they expected in a comprehensive breast center and how it should be organized from the patient's perspective. I knew what needed to be done medically, but I wanted the Bosom Buddies to guide us through all of the other aspects.

Once we had a good grasp of what the Bosom Buddies expected, we invited a group of fifteen general surgeons, who were doing the majority of the breast surgery in Fort Worth, to a meeting. We presented the idea of a comprehensive breast center to them along with several pages of suggestions from the Bosom Buddies. A few of the surgeons—fortunately not all—had the attitude, "We don't care that patients are going to Dallas or somewhere else for care. Let them go. We'll just take care of those who stay here."

Most remained interested in the concept and became the core group who ultimately organized and participated in the center. We had at least six meetings with them before the organizational structure of the new center was developed.

As soon as we had a consensus from them, we met with oncologists, then radiologists, and finally plastic surgeons. The pathologists were on board from the start. The entire process required two years of meetings and discussion.

Building on this group, the hospital CEO began the search for more surgeons, pathologists, radiologists, oncologists, and plastic surgeons who would be eager and willing to participate in this unique concept. It was not a simple task, because persuading docs to agree on anything other than their intense hatred of insurance companies is difficult at best.

There was also the *minor* issue of funding. We needed $3.4 million to build the center and finance its first three years of operation. Since the center would produce no revenue—its services would be free to all—another $10 million endowment would be necessary for the breast care center to be entirely self-sustaining.

In the fall of 2007, after dozens of meetings with physicians, administrators, and planners, we had assembled the core concepts that would constitute the new breast center. Now we needed a name for it before serious fund-raising could begin.

For me the naming was easy. When it came to breast cancer, Joan had been more unselfish with her time than anyone in our part of the state. Her very public struggle with the disease, coupled with her dedication and selfless personality, made her the obvious choice. She had been treated in a center with coordinated services for breast cancer patients and felt that everyone deserved the same. I'd never told anyone except Jenny, but I'd made the decision years ago that if my dream were to come true, the center would be named after Joan. In the fall of 2007, I proposed the "Joan Katz Breast Center," and everyone agreed.

Joan, however, had no idea about the plan. I had intentionally waited until the concept was almost complete before talking with her. Having failed in the past, I wanted to make sure we were really going to have a breast center before I approached her. I talked to Joan and her husband, Howard, at a coffee shop in late 2007.

She didn't say yes right away. She and her husband are humble people and have never wanted any adulation. Also, Joan felt that she *hadn't* done more than anyone else; she believed there were far-more-deserving individuals who should be considered, but I knew differently. After two months of thought and reflection, Joan finally (but reluctantly) agreed to let us use her name. Once she had accepted, however, she dedicated every spare moment to the daily planning and construction of the breast center.

The Joan Katz Breast Center fund-raising campaign officially began in early 2008. In spite of the disaster that defined the United States economy during that time, the initial fund-raising was completed in May 2009 thanks to the generosity of breast cancer survivors, their families, and hundreds of interested residents. We had our $3.4 million. Plans were drawn and construction began in October 2009.

The Joan Katz Breast Center officially opened to serve the women of North Texas in April 2010. My promise to Peggy and Paige was fulfilled. By October 2010, the center had treated more than 600 breast cancer patients, a number that is growing every month.

October 2010

Jenny and I continue to live in the same house where I first saw my inverted nipple in the bathroom mirror. Harley, our beloved lab, still rules the roost, as she has done for the past eleven years. Her once chocolate-brown muzzle is graying, and she's a little slower getting out of the pool, but she participates in our morning walks with gusto and still sleeps wrapped around my head.

My Harley-Davidson sits in the garage, a daily reminder of more carefree days. The triplets are twelve now and growing up. Their dad always wants to know if I would consider switching back—he gets the Harley and I cope with three teenagers. I've told him many times, "A trade is a trade."

Paige is still my patient, and I see her every year. She's in her mid-twenties and is still struggling with her mom's death.

My daughter Julie married Marc, and we have a beautiful blonde-haired granddaughter, Sydney Alan. She's the highlight of our lives—better than anything that's happened to us so far.

Jessica became an attorney and practices with a firm in Dallas. She has succeeded despite spending her high school years engulfed with the daily mess of a father suffering from breast cancer, chemo-hell, and hot flashes.

Many of the ideas about the breast center came from Jenny, although she would never take credit. She spends her mornings walking Harley and playing golf. She grabs Sydney for a long weekend every chance she gets, still tries growing tomatoes in our pathetic little garden, and simply enjoys life. And she still thinks I'm largely full of shit!

Whether it's my inborn ability to ignore things or just outright stupidity, I consider myself cured of breast cancer. Sydney needs grandpa to teach her to hunt, fish, and play golf. Harley needs to walk and swim. I need to keep learning about my profession. And there's golf to be played, fish to be caught, and old friends to spend time with. I figure I did enough worrying already.

But the scar across my chest that looks back at me every morning in the mirror serves as a stark reminder of what might have been, and that's pretty sobering. Before my cancer, I figured (as most of us do) that I was bulletproof. All that bad stuff I saw in the office every day happened to other folks, not to me.

Cancer is a great equalizer and a great teacher.

I was scared to death for several years, but now I just try to do my best every day and have fun doing it. I'm on a mission to learn everything I can about everything. I want to be eighty years old and still having an intelligent (and intelligible) conversation with Jenny, my kids, Sydney, and any other grandchildren that come along. If cancer comes again, I'll cope with it then, just like everyone else does. In the meantime, I refuse to worry about it.

I love my life, job, and family. What more could someone want? In August 2010, Jenny and I celebrated our fortieth wedding anniversary. I wouldn't have made it this far without her.

April 2011

We lost Harley this month. Metastatic splenic sarcoma. Only a few short days elapsed from the discovery of her tumor until we had to let her go. Not nearly enough time to say goodbye.

She had burst into our lives--a tiny, chocolate-brown bundle of unbridled joy, happiness, and enthusiasm--just as we found ourselves slipping into the depths of the cancer abyss. She wiggled, grinned, and licked her way into our hearts in a way no one could have anticipated. In her own special way, she made our journey infinitely more tolerable.

As I gagged my way to the porcelain throne during those despicable days after chemotherapy, she sat beside me. "It's OK, I'm here," streamed from her big, brown eyes. Every hot flash was eagerly licked away. Every time fear wedged itself into my thoughts, she flashed her wide, sloppy grin and let out a bark as if to say, "come on, Daddy, let's go swimming, take a run, walk, chase squirrels, anything! Life's too short to sit." When I couldn't sleep, she laid down next to me, put her muzzle on my neck, and let out a big sigh. She rubbed her cold wet nose on my cheek as if to say, "I understand. I'm here."

She was my friend and my running buddy throughout the entire "cancer thing," right up until that cool, clear, beautiful Thursday morning in April when we took our last walk together.

This book is dedicated to Harley Johns; she helped us through some extraordinarily rough times.

Jenny, Julie, Jessica, and I will miss her.

What You Need to Know if You Are Diagnosed With Breast Cancer

"I'm sorry, but your biopsy shows breast cancer."

What now?

First, and most important, remember that breast cancer is NOT an automatic death sentence! When properly treated, it is most often curable. Here is what you need to know or find out.

1. Your breast cancer diagnosis is a psychological emergency, not a medical one.

You must take enough time to make decisions that are right for you. Unless you have *inflammatory* breast cancer, the cancer will not grow rapidly enough over a few weeks to make any health difference. However, the decisions you make in the next seventy-two hours may truly determine whether you survive or not. Make these decisions slowly and wisely, and only after your terror has subsided a bit. Taking two to four weeks to get the right health team together and deciding what plan of action you need to take is not going to hurt you or make a difference in your outcome.

2. What type of breast cancer do you have?

Get a copy of the pathology report from your biopsy. This should be very simple; the doctor who did the biopsy will have it. Having a copy will save you a lot of time when you see a surgeon. Prepare yourself, however, for what you are going to read. Seeing your name in the "patient name" field directly next to the diagnosis "carcinoma" is psychologically devastating. I promise that it will hit you hard.

Get a three-ring binder and collect a copy of EVERY mammogram, CT or MRI scan, operative report, pathology report, laboratory report, and doctor's note as soon as they are available. Keep them arranged in chronological order. Take the notebook with you to every doctor visit. I assure you that it will be the ONLY complete record of your care.

3. Where do you go for advice?

What doctor do you see first? This is a particularly hard question to answer. Your best friend, your family doctor, your gynecologist, or your spouse may be a great source of support, but they may not really know about a surgeon. The surgeon's knowledge of the current treatment of breast cancer, surgical training, actual skill, expertise, and experience with breast cancer surgery, as well as the team of other specialists with whom they work and the hospital where they operate, are critical.

When someone suggests a doctor to you, there's a good chance you'll hear something like: "He is a good doctor. I really like him. Everyone goes to him." Those statements may be correct, but they're absolutely not the same as, "She knows what she's doing and she's the best-trained doctor for your problem." Personality counts when you're out for dinner but not

necessarily in the operating room. Some of the most skilled surgeons with whom I have had the privilege of operating possess
the personality of a pit bull. Remember, you don't want to be
their best friend, you want to survive.

4. How do you choose a surgeon?

Look for a general surgeon who has completed subspecialty
training in surgical oncology, including a breast oncology
fellowship. Go to the Society of Surgical Oncology website,
http://www.surgonc.org, and review the "Interdisciplinary
Breast Fellowship Core Educational Objectives," which out-
line the training required to complete a Society of Surgical
Oncology breast fellowship. It's an excellent guide for what
your surgeon should know.

**5. Once your surgeon has suggested a course of treatment,
always consider a second opinion from another surgeon who
meets the above criteria.**

There will always be some differences in doctors' recommendations, but they should be minimal. When you hear the same
advice twice, it's probably right. *Then* go for the best personality.

Remember, a second opinion is meant to make certain that
you are getting the same recommendations twice. Do not—I
repeat loudly, DO NOT—keep seeking opinions until you hear
what you want to hear. I promise that someone will tell you what
you want to hear, regardless of how stupid it might be.

**6. If possible, go to a comprehensive breast center that has
been accredited by the National Accreditation Program for
Breast Centers (NAPBC).**

The NAPBC is a relatively new, nongovernmental, not-for-profit organization that has been established to identify and recognize breast centers that provide quality care in the United States. For detailed information about the NAPBC, visit its website: http://www.accreditedbreastcenters.org.

7. Always take someone with you to doctor visits.

Thanks to thousands of important discussions with patients, I learned that regardless of how hard I tried, how long I took, and how detailed my discussion was, my patients usually absorbed only a choice few words. Cancer, STD, pregnant, abnormal, and ovarian mass are words that seem to stick in patients' minds and effectively plug their ears to everything that follows. They hear little else. A spouse, relative, or friend accompanying you can be invaluable when you get home and try to accurately remember what was said.

8. Utilize the services of a "nurse navigator," preferably one certified by the Breast Patient Navigator Certification Program, a program of the National Consortium of Breast Centers (NCBC).

The program's website is http://www.bpnc.org.

A nurse navigator can be a voice of hope, help, and reason when the world seems to be crashing around you.

9. There is absolutely, positively NO "natural" cure for breast cancer.

If cancer could be cured with a diet of tree bark, Johnson grass, apricot pits, and moist newspaper, no one would die of the disease. Every doctor in the world would jump on that bandwagon. If you have breast cancer and are told that you can survive by taking "natural," "bioidentical," "nontoxic," or "gentle" treatment, it's total nonsense. These products may not do any harm, but they don't do any good, either.

If your doctor proposes a regimen to treat any of the following, be wary:

- Weak immune system
- Lack of oxygen to the cells
- Excessive toxins
- Too much or too little acidity
- Colon toxins
- Heavy metal toxicity

Also be very suspicious about any of the following terms; they can be a very expensive way to accomplish nothing:

- Natural
- Holistic
- Bioenergy healing
- Energy fields
- Probiotic

10. If you can't find a proposed treatment on the websites of the Society of Surgical Oncology, the American Cancer Society, the American College of Surgeons, or the American Society of Breast Surgeons, then most likely it has never been proved to be safe and/or effective. That's about the same thing as saying, "It doesn't work."

According to James Randi, "alternative medicine" appeals to people's childish nature. Alternative medicine promises all benefit and no risk, all cures and no failures, and treatment of the deadliest diseases human beings face without side effects or pain. Who wouldn't think that's appealing? However, these promises are the very embodiment of the maxim that says, "If it sounds too good to be true, it almost certainly is."

If "alternative medicine" actually cured breast cancer, there should be dozens of peer-reviewed, randomized, double-blind, controlled clinical trials comparing the "alternative" treatment (no matter what it is) and conventional therapy. These studies should be published in well-established, reputable, peer-reviewed specialty journals such as the *Journal of the American College of Surgeons*, the *Journal of the National Cancer Institute*, the *New England Journal of Medicine*, or numerous others of similar reputation. Quite simply, there are none, repeat, none. No such studies exist, and there is certainly a reason for that.

The reality is that no "alternative" or "homeopathic" treatment for breast cancer has *ever* proved successful in rigorously controlled trials. In fact, none has performed any better than placebos. Once a treatment has proved safe *and* effective, it is no longer called "alternative"; it's called "medicine."

When word of your condition leaks out, friends (and people who think they're your friends) will invariably try to help with some of the most ridiculous suggestions imaginable. They don't mean any harm; they just don't have a clue what they are talking about. If a friend suggests that you treat your breast cancer "naturally," remember a quote from James Randi: "Bird shit and gravel are all-natural, too, but I don't eat them."

11. Lifestyle changes help everything. There is no question that both weight loss (if you are overweight or obese) and exercise are beneficial to your long-term health.

The better your physical condition when you are diagnosed with cancer (no matter what type), the better your chances of survival become. The time for lifestyle changes is before bad stuff happens, but it certainly helps even afterward.

Diet and exercise are always beneficial, but they are not primary treatments for breast cancer. They're very good for the psyche, good for mental health and toughness, but cancer cells don't care how fast you can run a mile.

12. Knowledge is power.

Learn about your disease and your treatment, and stay informed. Always seek scientifically sound and reliable information. Look for credible, reputable websites that are sponsored by well-recognized, national organizations dedicated to the diagnosis and treatment of breast disease.

13. Communicate with your medical team.

They can and will answer your questions and help you manage your situation. They won't know you're having problems unless you tell them.

Most of all, remember: This is a journey, but it's a marathon, not a sprint.

Photos from the Journey

Alan and Harley celebrating the end of Tamoxifen and hot flashes

Sydney Alan, Marc, and Julie Schmidt

Jessica Johns, age fifteen, on my "traded for triplets" Harley-Davidson

Jenny and Harley

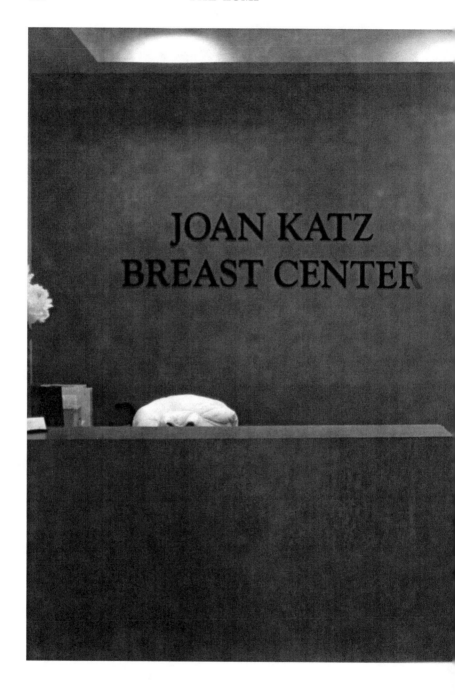

© David Lozak

The Joan Katz Breast Center. Joan's photo was taken just prior to the opening.

Dance of Life *sculpted by Michael Pavlovsky and donated to the*
Joan Katz Breast Center

CPSIA information can be obtained at www.ICGtesting.com
Printed in the USA
LVOW080416210512

282547LV00001B/88/P